THE PLANT-BASED DIET WOK COOKBOOK

By

JANE F. GARRAWAY

Copyright © 2024

Copyright © 2024 by Jane F. Garraway

TABLE OF CONTENTS

PLANT-BASED DIET 101

In a world where health and sustainability are connected, the plant-based diet emerges as a beacon of balanced nutrition and mindful living. This chapter delves into the essence of plant-based eating, introducing you to its principles, benefits, and the abundant variety of foods that compose this lifestyle.

The Essence of Plant-Based Eating

At its core, a plant-based diet revolves around consuming foods primarily derived from plants. This includes fruits, vegetables, legumes, whole grains, nuts, and seeds. The emphasis is on whole, unprocessed foods that provide essential nutrients and promote overall well-being. Unlike vegetarian or vegan diets, plant-based eating encourages a conscious reduction in animal products without eliminating them entirely.

The Benefits

Plant-based eating offers a plethora of health advantages. Rich in fiber, vitamins, and minerals, this diet can aid in weight management, lower cholesterol levels, and reduce the risk of chronic diseases such as heart disease, type 2 diabetes, and certain cancers. The high antioxidant content of plant-based foods contributes to the body's defense against oxidative stress and inflammation.

Nutritional Essentials

Understanding the key nutrients in a plant-based diet is essential for maintaining optimal health. Protein, iron, calcium, vitamin B12, omega-3 fatty acids, and zinc are vital components that may require special attention. Learning to incorporate diverse plant sources to meet these nutritional needs is a cornerstone of successful plant-based living.

Embracing Diversity

One of the remarkable aspects of a plant-based diet is its diversity. Explore the rainbow of colors and flavors that nature offers through a wide range of fruits and vegetables. Dive into hearty legumes like lentils, chickpeas, and beans, which provide protein and fiber. Discover the versatility of whole grains like quinoa, brown rice, and oats that serve as nutrient-rich bases for various dishes.

Transitioning Gracefully

For beginners, transitioning gradually can be a practical approach. Start by replacing a few meals a week with plant-based options, and gradually increase the ratio of plant foods on your plate. This approach allows your taste buds to adapt and ensures a sustainable shift towards a more plant-focused lifestyle.

Cultivating Awareness

Beyond the personal benefits, adopting a plant-based diet contributes to the preservation of our environment. The reduction in animal agriculture lessens the carbon footprint and promotes sustainability. By making mindful choices about what we eat, we actively participate in the global effort to create a more sustainable and compassionate world.

As you embark on your journey into the world of plant-based nutrition, keep an open mind and a curious spirit. Each meal is an opportunity to nourish your body and embrace the vitality that plant-based foods offer.

Benefits of Plant-Based Diet: Why You Should Give It a Try

The allure of a plant-based diet extends far beyond the realm of health, permeating into various aspects of your life and the world around you. In this chapter, we'll uncover the diverse array of benefits that make embracing plant-based eating a transformative and rewarding choice.

Promotes Heart Health

Plant-based diets are inherently low in saturated fats and cholesterol, which are often linked to heart disease. The abundance of fiber, antioxidants, and healthy fats found in plant foods can help lower blood pressure, reduce bad cholesterol levels, and decrease the risk of heart-related issues.

Aids Weight Management

Plant-based diets tend to be naturally lower in calories while being rich in fiber, which helps control appetite and promote feelings of fullness. This combination can support weight loss and maintenance goals, without compromising on essential nutrients.

Reduces Chronic Disease Risk

Numerous studies suggest that a plant-based diet can reduce the risk of chronic diseases such as type 2 diabetes, certain cancers, and hypertension. The anti-inflammatory properties of plant foods play a significant role in protecting cells from damage and maintaining overall health.

Boosts Energy and Vitality

Plant-based foods are packed with essential vitamins, minerals, and phytonutrients that provide a sustained source of energy. Their ability to improve digestion and support the body's natural detoxification processes contributes to enhanced vitality and overall well-being.

Environmental Sustainability

By shifting towards a plant-based diet, you contribute to reducing the demand for resource-intensive animal agriculture. This has a positive impact on reducing greenhouse gas emissions, conserving water, and preserving natural ecosystems, ultimately supporting a more sustainable planet.

Ethical Considerations

Choosing a plant-based lifestyle aligns with ethical concerns about animal welfare. By reducing or eliminating animal product consumption, you actively support the prevention of animal suffering and exploitation, fostering a sense of compassion and empathy.

Culinary Adventure

Exploring plant-based cuisine introduces you to an exciting world of flavors, textures, and culinary creativity. The diverse array of fruits, vegetables, grains, legumes, and nuts offers endless possibilities for crafting delicious and satisfying meals.

Empowerment Through Choice

Opting for a plant-based diet empowers you to make conscious decisions about what you put on your plate. By taking control of your dietary choices, you take a step towards self-care and personal growth.

Connection to Nature

Embracing plant-based eating encourages a deeper connection with nature and its cycles. It reminds us of our interconnectedness with the environment and reinforces the notion that our dietary choices have far-reaching consequences.

A Path Towards Wellness

Incorporating more plant-based foods into your diet is not about restriction; it's about abundance, nourishment, and holistic well-being. By prioritizing whole, plant-derived foods, you create a foundation for lifelong health and a positive impact on the world around you.

As you embark on your plant-based journey, remember that every meal you choose is an opportunity to nourish yourself and contribute to a better future. The benefits are multi-faceted, touching on health, the environment, ethics, and personal empowerment. The upcoming chapters will guide you through practical steps to embrace a plant-based lifestyle, from meal planning and grocery shopping to mastering flavorful recipes that will become staples in your culinary repertoire.

Plant-Based Diet Vs. Vegan Diet Vs. Vegetarian Diet

In the realm of dietary choices, plant-based, vegan, and vegetarian diets stand out as distinctive paths that prioritize different levels of animal product consumption. This chapter will clarify the nuances between these diets, shedding light on their motivations, restrictions, and potential benefits.

Plant-Based Diet

A plant-based diet is characterized by its emphasis on whole, plant-derived foods. While animal products might be consumed occasionally, they are not the focal point of meals. This approach places a premium on fruits, vegetables, legumes, nuts, seeds, and whole grains. The primary motivation behind adopting a plant-based diet often includes improved health, reduced environmental impact, and a preference for ethical treatment of animals.

Vegan Diet

Veganism extends the plant-based philosophy to its furthest extent. A vegan diet strictly excludes all animal products, including meat, dairy, eggs, and even honey. This ethical lifestyle choice aims to eliminate the use of animals for food, clothing, and other purposes. Veganism is driven by principles of animal welfare, environmental conservation, and human health. Individuals adopting a vegan diet need to be mindful of potential nutritional gaps, such as vitamin B12 and omega-3 fatty acids, and ensure adequate supplementation or sourcing from fortified foods.

Vegetarian Diet

A vegetarian diet abstains from meat but may include other animal products such as dairy and eggs. This category encompasses various subtypes, including lacto-vegetarian (consumes dairy), ovo-vegetarian (consumes eggs), and lacto-ovo-vegetarian (consumes both dairy and eggs). The motivations behind adopting a vegetarian diet can range from ethical concerns to health considerations.

Comparing and Contrasting

- **Animal Product Consumption**: Plant-based and vegan diets minimize or eliminate animal products entirely, while vegetarian diets vary in the inclusion of dairy and/or eggs.

- **Health Focus:** All three diets can support improved health when based on whole, nutrient-dense foods. However, a poorly planned vegetarian or vegan diet may lack certain essential nutrients, highlighting the importance of proper nutritional knowledge.

- **Ethical and Environmental Concerns:** Plant-based and vegan diets align closely with ethical concerns related to animal welfare and environmental sustainability. Vegetarian diets may address these concerns to a lesser extent, depending on the specific choices made within the diet.

- **Nutritional Considerations**: All diets must be well-balanced to ensure adequate intake of nutrients such as protein, iron, calcium, vitamin B12, and omega-3 fatty acids. Individuals should be aware of potential deficiencies and take steps to meet their nutritional needs through diverse food choices or supplements.

Choosing the right diet for you involves careful consideration of your values, health goals, and dietary preferences. Understanding the differences between plant-based, vegan, and vegetarian diets empowers you to make informed decisions that resonate with your individual lifestyle and values.

CURRY & SOUP

Cauliflower and Potato Curry

A hearty and flavorful vegan dish.

 **Prep Time:** 15 minutes || **Cook Time:** 20 minutes || **Yield:** 4 servings

INGREDIENTS

For the curry paste:

- 1/4 cup curry powder

- 1 tablespoon ground cumin

- 1 teaspoon ground coriander

- 1/2 teaspoon turmeric

- 1/4 teaspoon red pepper flakes (adjust to taste)

- 1/4 cup coconut milk

For the stir-fry:

- 1 tablespoon vegetable oil

- 1 onion, thinly sliced

- 2 cloves garlic, minced

- 1 inch piece ginger, grated

- 1 medium cauliflower, cut into florets

- 1 medium potato, cubed

- 1 can (14.5 oz) coconut milk

- 1/4 cup vegetable broth

- 1 tablespoon soy sauce or tamari

- 1 teaspoon honey or maple syrup

- 1/4 cup chopped cilantro

INSTRUCTIONS

1. In a small bowl, combine the curry powder, cumin, coriander, turmeric, red pepper flakes, and coconut milk. Stir until well combined.

2. Heat a wok or large skillet over high heat. Add the vegetable oil.

3. Add the onion, garlic, and ginger to the wok. Stir-fry for 1-2 minutes, or until fragrant.

4. Add the cauliflower florets and potato cubes to the wok. Stir-fry for 3-4 minutes, or until slightly softened.

5. Add the curry paste to the wok. Stir-fry for 1 minute, or until fragrant.

6. Add the coconut milk and vegetable broth to the wok. Bring to a simmer.

7. Simmer the curry until the vegetables are tender and the sauce has thickened, about 10-15 minutes.

8. Stir in the soy sauce, rice vinegar, and honey. Adjust the seasoning to taste. Garnish with chopped cilantro and serve immediately over rice.

NOTES

- For a spicier curry, add more red pepper flakes.

- To make this dish gluten-free, use tamari instead of soy sauce.

- Serve with a side of naan bread or rice for a complete meal.

NUTRITIONAL INFO (approximate, per serving)

- Calories: 350-400 | Protein: 15-20g | Fat: 20-25g | Carbohydrates: 30-35g | Fiber: 5-7g | Net Carbs: 25-30g

Plant-Based Wonton Soup

A hearty and flavorful vegan soup.

 **Prep Time:** 30 minutes || **Cook Time:** 15 minutes || **Yield:** 4 servings

INGREDIENTS

For the wonton wrappers:

- 1 package wonton wrappers

- 1/2 cup plant-based ground meat (soy, pea, or lentil)

- 1/4 cup chopped scallions

- 1 tablespoon soy sauce or tamari

- 1 teaspoon grated ginger

- 1/4 teaspoon garlic powder

- 1/4 teaspoon red pepper flakes

For the broth:

- 4 cups vegetable broth

- 1 onion, quartered

- 1 carrot, chopped

- 1 stalk celery, chopped

- 1 inch piece ginger, sliced

- 1 clove garlic, minced

- 1 tablespoon soy sauce or tamari

- 1 teaspoon rice vinegar

- 1/2 teaspoon sesame oil

For the stir-fry:

- 1 tablespoon vegetable oil

- 1/4 cup chopped scallions

- 1/4 cup shredded carrots

- 1/4 cup snow peas

INSTRUCTIONS

1. In a bowl, combine the plant-based ground meat, chopped scallions, soy sauce, ginger, garlic powder, and red pepper flakes. Mix well. Place a small amount of the mixture in the center of each wonton wrapper. Fold the wrappers diagonally and seal the edges by pressing firmly.

2. In a large pot, combine the vegetable broth, onion, carrot, celery, ginger, and garlic. Bring to a boil, then reduce heat and simmer for 30 minutes. Strain the broth and discard the vegetables.

3. Heat a wok or large skillet over high heat. Add the vegetable oil. Stir-fry the scallions, carrots, and snow peas for 2-3 minutes, or until crisp-tender.

4. Add the wontons to the boiling broth. Cook for 3-5 minutes, or until the wontons float to the surface and are cooked through.

5. Add the soy sauce, rice vinegar, and sesame oil to the broth. Taste and adjust seasonings as needed.

6. Serve the soup hot, topped with the stir-fried vegetables.

NOTES

- For a spicier soup, add more red pepper flakes to the wonton filling or broth.

- To make this dish gluten-free, use tamari instead of soy sauce.

- Serve with additional scallions or other garnishes, such as chopped cilantro or sesame seeds.

NUTRITIONAL INFO (approximate, per serving)

- Calories: 300-350 | Protein: 20-25g | Fat: 15-20g | Carbohydrates: 20-25g | Fiber: 5-7g | Net Carbs: 15-18g

Thai Red Curry with Tofu

A flavorful and aromatic vegan dish.

 **Prep Time:** 15 minutes || **Cook Time:** 10 minutes || **Yield:** 4 servings

INGREDIENTS

For the marinade:

- 1 block extra-firm tofu, pressed and cubed
- 1 tablespoon soy sauce or tamari
- 1 teaspoon rice vinegar
- 1/2 teaspoon cornstarch
- 1/4 teaspoon red pepper flakes
- 1/4 teaspoon garlic powder
- 1/4 teaspoon ginger powder

For the curry:

- 1 tablespoon vegetable oil
- 1 onion, thinly sliced
- 2 cloves garlic, minced
- 1 inch piece ginger, grated
- 1 can (14.5 oz) coconut milk
- 1/4 cup red curry paste
- 1 tablespoon soy sauce or tamari
- 1 tablespoon rice vinegar
- 1 teaspoon honey or maple syrup
- 1/2 teaspoon red pepper flakes
- 1/4 cup chopped basil

INSTRUCTIONS

1. In a bowl, combine the tofu cubes with the marinade ingredients. Toss to coat and let marinate for at least 15 minutes, or up to 30 minutes.

2. Heat a wok or large skillet over high heat. Add the vegetable oil.

3. Add the onion, garlic, and ginger to the wok. Stir-fry for 1-2 minutes, or until fragrant.

4. Add the red curry paste to the wok. Stir-fry for 1 minute, or until fragrant.

5. Add the coconut milk to the wok. Bring to a simmer.

6. Add the marinated tofu to the wok. Stir-fry for 3-4 minutes, or until browned and heated through.

7. Add the soy sauce, rice vinegar, honey, and red pepper flakes to the wok. Stir-fry for 1 minute more, or until everything is coated in the sauce. Sprinkle with chopped basil and serve immediately over rice.

NOTES

- For a spicier curry, use a hotter red curry paste or add more red pepper flakes.

- To make this dish gluten-free, use tamari instead of soy sauce.

- Serve over brown rice or cauliflower rice for a complete meal.

NUTRITIONAL INFO (approximate, per serving)

- Calories: 350-400 | Protein: 20-25g | Fat: 20-25g | Carbohydrates: 20-25g | Fiber: 5-7g | Net Carbs: 15-18g

Singapore Curry Noodles

A flavorful and spicy vegan dish.

 **Prep Time:** 15 minutes || **Cook Time:** 10 minutes || **Yield:** 4 servings

INGREDIENTS

For the stir-fry:

- 1 tablespoon vegetable oil

- 1 onion, thinly sliced

- 2 cloves garlic, minced

- 1 inch piece ginger, grated

- 1/2 cup broccoli florets

- 1/2 cup carrots, thinly sliced

- 1/4 cup snow peas

- 1/4 cup red bell pepper, thinly sliced

- 8 ounces rice noodles (wide)

- 1/4 cup curry paste

- 1/4 cup coconut milk

- 2 tablespoons soy sauce or tamari

- 1 tablespoon rice vinegar

- 1 teaspoon honey or maple syrup

INSTRUCTIONS

1. Cook the rice noodles. Drain and set aside.

2. Heat a wok or large skillet over high heat. Add the vegetable oil.

3. Add the onion, garlic, and ginger to the wok. Stir-fry for 1-2 minutes, or until fragrant.

4. Add the broccoli, carrots, snow peas, and red bell pepper to the wok. Stir-fry for 3-4 minutes, or until crisp-tender.

5. Add the cooked rice noodles to the wok. Break them apart with a spatula and stir-fry for 2-3 minutes, or until heated through.

6. Add the curry paste, coconut milk, soy sauce, rice vinegar, and honey to the wok. Stir-fry for 1 minute, or until the sauce is heated through.

7. Combine the vegetables, noodles, and sauce. Stir-fry for 1 minute more, or until everything is coated in the sauce. Serve immediately.

NOTES

- For a spicier dish, use a hotter curry paste or add red pepper flakes.

- To make this dish gluten-free, use tamari instead of soy sauce.

- Serve with a side of stir-fried vegetables or a salad for a complete meal.

NUTRITIONAL INFO (approximate, per serving)

- Calories: 350-400 | Protein: 15-20g | Fat: 15-20g | Carbohydrates: 30-35g | Fiber: 5-7g | Net Carbs: 25-30g

Thai Panang Curry with Tofu

A flavorful and aromatic vegan dish.

 **Prep Time:** 15 minutes || **Cook Time:** 10 minutes || **Yield:** 4 servings

INGREDIENTS

For the marinade:

- 1 block extra-firm tofu, pressed and cubed

- 1 tablespoon soy sauce or tamari

- 1 teaspoon rice vinegar

- 1/2 teaspoon cornstarch

- 1/4 teaspoon red pepper flakes

- 1/4 teaspoon garlic powder

- 1/4 teaspoon ginger powder

For the curry paste:

- 1/4 cup red curry paste

- 1 tablespoon coconut milk

- 1 teaspoon sugar

- 1/2 teaspoon fish sauce (can be substituted with tamari)

For the stir-fry:

- 1 tablespoon vegetable oil

- 1 onion, thinly sliced

- 2 cloves garlic, minced

- 1 inch piece ginger, grated

- 1 can (14.5 oz) coconut milk

- 1/4 cup vegetable broth

- 1 tablespoon soy sauce or tamari

- 1 teaspoon rice vinegar

- 1 teaspoon honey or maple syrup

- 1/2 teaspoon red pepper flakes

- 1/4 cup chopped basil

INSTRUCTIONS

1. In a bowl, combine the tofu cubes with the marinade ingredients. Toss to coat and let marinate for at least 15 minutes, or up to 30 minutes.

2. In a small bowl, combine the red curry paste, coconut milk, sugar, and fish sauce.

3. Heat a wok or large skillet over high heat. Add the vegetable oil.

4. Add the onion, garlic, and ginger to the wok. Stir-fry for 1-2 minutes, or until fragrant.

5. Add the curry paste to the wok. Stir-fry for 1 minute, or until fragrant.

6. Add the coconut milk and vegetable broth to the wok. Bring to a simmer.

7. Add the marinated tofu to the wok. Stir-fry for 3-4 minutes, or until browned and heated through.

8. Add the soy sauce, rice vinegar, honey, and red pepper flakes to the wok. Stir-fry for 1 minute more, or until everything is coated in the sauce. Sprinkle with chopped basil and serve immediately over rice.

NOTES

- For a spicier curry, use a hotter red curry paste or add more red pepper flakes.

- To make this dish gluten-free, use tamari instead of soy sauce.

- Serve over brown rice or cauliflower rice for a complete meal.

NUTRITIONAL INFO (approximate, per serving)

- Calories: 350-400 | Protein: 20-25g | Fat: 20-25g | Carbohydrates: 20-25g | Fiber: 5-7g | Net Carbs: 15-18g

Keerai Thengai Curry (Spinach Coconut Curry)

A creamy and flavorful South Indian curry.

 **Prep Time:** 15 minutes || **Cook Time:** 20 minutes || **Yield:** 4 servings

INGREDIENTS

- 1 bunch spinach, chopped

- 1/2 cup grated coconut

- 1 tablespoon coconut oil

- 1/2 teaspoon mustard seeds

- 1 dry red chili, broken into pieces

- 1 pinch asafoetida powder

- 1/4 teaspoon turmeric powder

- 1/4 teaspoon salt

- 1/4 cup water

INSTRUCTIONS

1. In a wok or large skillet, heat the coconut oil over medium heat. Add the mustard seeds and let them sizzle until they start to pop.

2. Add the dry red chili, asafoetida powder, turmeric powder, and salt. Stir for a few seconds.

3. Add the chopped spinach to the wok. Stir-fry until the spinach wilts and the water has evaporated.

4. In a blender, grind the grated coconut with a little water until smooth.

5. Add the coconut paste to the wok and stir well. Cook for a few minutes, or until the flavors have combined.

6. Add the water and simmer for a few minutes, or until the curry has thickened.

7. Serve hot as a main course or side dish.

NOTES

- For a spicier curry, add more red chili or a pinch of cayenne pepper.

- You can substitute spinach with other leafy greens like kale, collard greens, or fenugreek leaves.

NUTRITIONAL INFO (approximate, per serving)

- Calories: 200-250 | Protein: 5-7g | Fat: 15-20g | Carbohydrates: 15-20g | Fiber: 3-5g | Net Carbs: 10-15g

SAUCES

Szechuan Stir-Fry Sauce

A flavorful and spicy sauce for your vegan stir-fries.

 **Yields:** About 1/4 cup

INGREDIENTS

- 1/4 cup soy sauce or tamari

- 2 tablespoons rice vinegar

- 1 tablespoon honey or maple syrup

- 1 tablespoon chili oil

- 1 teaspoon Sichuan peppercorns, ground

- 1/2 teaspoon red pepper flakes

- 1 clove garlic, minced

- 1/2 teaspoon ginger, grated

INSTRUCTIONS

1. In a small bowl, whisk together the soy sauce, rice vinegar, honey, chili oil, Sichuan peppercorns, red pepper flakes, garlic, and ginger.

2. Taste the sauce and adjust the ingredients to your liking.

NOTES

- For a spicier sauce, add more chili oil, Sichuan peppercorns, or red pepper flakes.

- To make this sauce gluten-free, use tamari instead of soy sauce.

- This sauce can be used to marinate tofu, tempeh, or vegetables before stir-frying.

NUTRITIONAL INFO (approximate, per serving)

- Calories: 50-75 | Protein: 1-2g | Fat: 5-8g | Carbohydrates: 5-8g | Fiber: 1-2g | Net Carbs: 3-5g

Zhoug Cilantro-Jalapeno Stir-Fry Sauce

A flavorful and spicy sauce for your vegan stir-fries.

 **Yields:** About 1/4 cup

INGREDIENTS

- 1/4 cup cilantro, chopped

- 2 jalapeños, seeded and chopped

- 2 cloves garlic

- 1 tablespoon olive oil

- 1 tablespoon lemon juice

- 1/2 teaspoon cumin

- 1/4 teaspoon salt

INSTRUCTIONS

1. In a food processor or blender, combine the cilantro, jalapeños, garlic, olive oil, lemon juice, cumin, and salt.

2. Blend or pulse until the ingredients are finely chopped and the sauce is smooth.

3. Taste the sauce and adjust the ingredients to your liking.

NOTES

- For a spicier sauce, leave the seeds in the jalapeños.

- This sauce can be used to marinate tofu, tempeh, or vegetables before stir-frying.

- Serve over rice or noodles for a complete meal.

NUTRITIONAL INFO (approximate, per serving)

- Calories: 50-75 | Protein: 1-2g | Fat: 5-8g | Carbohydrates: 5-8g | Fiber: 1-2g | Net Carbs: 3-5g

Sweet and Spicy Stir-Fry Sauce

A versatile sauce for your vegan stir-fries.

**Yields:** About 1/4 cup

INGREDIENTS

- 1/4 cup ketchup

- 1/4 cup pineapple juice

- 2 tablespoons rice vinegar

- 1 tablespoon honey or maple syrup

- 1 tablespoon chili oil

- 1/4 teaspoon red pepper flakes

INSTRUCTIONS

1. In a small bowl, whisk together the ketchup, pineapple juice, rice vinegar, honey, chili oil, and red pepper flakes.

2. Taste the sauce and adjust the ingredients to your liking.

NOTES

- For a spicier sauce, add more chili oil or red pepper flakes.

- This sauce can be used to marinate tofu, tempeh, or vegetables before stir-frying.

NUTRITIONAL INFO (approximate, per serving)

- Calories: 50-75 | Protein: 1-2g | Fat: 5-8g | Carbohydrates: 10-15g | Fiber: 0-1g | Net Carbs: 9-14g

Teriyaki Stir-Fry Sauce

A sweet and savory sauce for your vegan stir-fries.

 **Yields:** About 1/4 cup

INGREDIENTS

- 1/4 cup soy sauce or tamari

- 2 tablespoons rice vinegar

- 1 tablespoon honey or maple syrup

- 1 tablespoon mirin (can be substituted with rice wine)

- 1/2 teaspoon grated ginger

- 1/4 teaspoon garlic powder

INSTRUCTIONS

1. In a small bowl, whisk together the soy sauce, rice vinegar, honey, mirin, ginger, and garlic powder.

2. Taste the sauce and adjust the ingredients to your liking.

NOTES

- For a spicier sauce, add red pepper flakes.

- To make this sauce gluten-free, use tamari instead of soy sauce.

- This sauce can be used to marinate tofu, tempeh, or vegetables before stir-frying.

NUTRITIONAL INFO (approximate, per serving)

- Calories: 50-75 | Protein: 1-2g | Fat: 5-8g | Carbohydrates: 5-8g | Fiber: 1-2g | Net Carbs: 3-5g

Thai Sweet Chili Stir-Fry Sauce

A flavorful and tangy sauce for your vegan stir-fries.

 **Yields:** About 1/4 cup

INGREDIENTS

- 1/4 cup sweet chili sauce

- 1 tablespoon soy sauce or tamari

- 1 tablespoon rice vinegar

- 1 teaspoon honey or maple syrup

- 1/4 teaspoon red pepper flakes (optional)

INSTRUCTIONS

1. In a small bowl, whisk together the sweet chili sauce, soy sauce, rice vinegar, honey, and red pepper flakes (if using).

2. Taste the sauce and adjust the ingredients to your liking.

NOTES

- For a spicier sauce, add more red pepper flakes.

- To make this sauce gluten-free, use tamari instead of soy sauce.

- This sauce can be used to marinate tofu, tempeh, or vegetables before stir-frying.

NUTRITIONAL INFO (approximate, per serving)

- Calories: 50-75 | Protein: 1-2g | Fat: 5-8g | Carbohydrates: 5-8g | Fiber: 1-2g | Net Carbs: 3-5g

Chinese Garlic Stir-Fry Sauce

A flavorful and versatile sauce for your vegan stir-fries.

**Yields:** About 1/4 cup

INGREDIENTS

- 1/4 cup soy sauce or tamari

- 2 tablespoons rice vinegar

- 1 tablespoon honey or maple syrup

- 2 cloves garlic, minced

- 1/2 teaspoon red pepper flakes (optional)

INSTRUCTIONS

1. In a small bowl, whisk together the soy sauce, rice vinegar, honey, garlic, and red pepper flakes (if using).

2. Taste the sauce and adjust the ingredients to your liking.

NOTES

- For a spicier sauce, add more red pepper flakes.

- To make this sauce gluten-free, use tamari instead of soy sauce.

- This sauce can be used to marinate tofu, tempeh, or vegetables before stir-frying.

NUTRITIONAL INFO (approximate, per serving)

- Calories: 50-75 | Protein: 1-2g | Fat: 5-8g | Carbohydrates: 5-8g | Fiber: 1-2g | Net Carbs: 3-5g

Miso Ginger Stir-Fry Sauce

A savory and flavorful sauce for your vegan stir-fries.

**Yields:** About 1/4 cup

INGREDIENTS

- 1/4 cup white miso paste

- 2 tablespoons rice vinegar

- 1 tablespoon honey or maple syrup

- 1 tablespoon sesame oil

- 1 clove garlic, minced

- 1 inch piece ginger, grated

INSTRUCTIONS

1. In a small bowl, whisk together the miso paste, rice vinegar, honey, sesame oil, garlic, and ginger.

2. Taste the sauce and adjust the ingredients to your liking. If the sauce is too thick, add a little water.

NOTES

- This sauce can be used to marinate tofu, tempeh, or vegetables before stir-frying.

- For a spicier sauce, add red pepper flakes.

- Serve over rice or noodles for a complete meal.

NUTRITIONAL INFO (approximate, per serving)

- Calories: 50-75 | Protein: 1-2g | Fat: 5-8g | Carbohydrates: 5-8g | Fiber: 1-2g | Net Carbs: 3-5g

Peri-Peri Stir-Fry Sauce

A spicy and flavorful sauce for your vegan stir-fries.

 **Yields:** About 1/4 cup

INGREDIENTS

- 1/4 cup peri-peri sauce

- 1 tablespoon soy sauce or tamari

- 1 tablespoon rice vinegar

- 1 teaspoon honey or maple syrup

- 1/2 teaspoon red pepper flakes (optional)

INSTRUCTIONS

1. In a small bowl, whisk together the peri-peri sauce, soy sauce, rice vinegar, honey, and red pepper flakes (if using).

2. Taste the sauce and adjust the ingredients to your liking.

NOTES

- For a spicier sauce, use a hotter peri-peri sauce or add more red pepper flakes.

- To make this sauce gluten-free, use tamari instead of soy sauce.

- This sauce can be used to marinate tofu, tempeh, or vegetables before stir-frying.

NUTRITIONAL INFO (approximate, per serving)

- Calories: 50-75 | Protein: 1-2g | Fat: 5-8g | Carbohydrates: 5-8g | Fiber: 1-2g | Net Carbs: 3-5g

Sweet and Sour Stir-Fry Sauce

A tangy and flavorful sauce for your vegan stir-fries.

 **Yields:** About 1/4 cup

INGREDIENTS

- 1/4 cup ketchup

- 1/4 cup pineapple juice

- 2 tablespoons rice vinegar

- 1 tablespoon sugar or honey

- 1 tablespoon cornstarch

- 1/4 teaspoon red pepper flakes (optional)

INSTRUCTIONS

1. In a small bowl, whisk together the ketchup, pineapple juice, rice vinegar, sugar, cornstarch, and red pepper flakes (if using).

2. Taste the sauce and adjust the ingredients to your liking.

NOTES

- For a spicier sauce, add more red pepper flakes.

- This sauce can be used to marinate tofu, tempeh, or vegetables before stir-frying.

NUTRITIONAL INFO (approximate, per serving)

- Calories: 50-75 | Protein: 1-2g | Fat: 0-1g | Carbohydrates: 10-15g | Fiber: 0-1g | Net Carbs: 9-14g

Lemon Tahini Stir-Fry Sauce

A tangy and flavorful sauce for your vegan stir-fries.

 **Yields:** About 1/4 cup

INGREDIENTS

- 1/4 cup tahini

- 2 tablespoons lemon juice

- 1 tablespoon soy sauce or tamari

- 1 tablespoon rice vinegar

- 1 tablespoon water

- 1 clove garlic, minced

- 1/2 teaspoon red pepper flakes (optional)

INSTRUCTIONS

1. In a small bowl, whisk together the tahini, lemon juice, soy sauce, rice vinegar, water, garlic, and red pepper flakes (if using).

2. Taste the sauce and adjust the ingredients to your liking. If the sauce is too thick, add more water.

NOTES

- For a spicier sauce, add more red pepper flakes.

- To make this sauce gluten-free, use tamari instead of soy sauce.

- This sauce can be used to marinate tofu, tempeh, or vegetables before stir-frying.

NUTRITIONAL INFO (approximate, per serving)

- Calories: 150-200 | Protein: 3-5g | Fat: 15-20g | Carbohydrates: 5-8g | Fiber: 1-2g | Net Carbs: 3-5g

Ginger-Garlic Stir-Fry Sauce

A flavorful and versatile sauce for your vegan stir-fries.

 **Yields:** About 1/4 cup

INGREDIENTS

- 1/4 cup soy sauce or tamari

- 2 tablespoons rice vinegar

- 1 tablespoon honey or maple syrup

- 2 cloves garlic, minced

- 1 inch piece ginger, grated

- 1/2 teaspoon red pepper flakes (optional)

INSTRUCTIONS

1. In a small bowl, whisk together the soy sauce, rice vinegar, honey, garlic, ginger, and red pepper flakes (if using).

2. Taste the sauce and adjust the ingredients to your liking.

NOTES

- For a spicier sauce, add more red pepper flakes.

- To make this sauce gluten-free, use tamari instead of soy sauce.

- This sauce can be used to marinate tofu, tempeh, or vegetables before stir-frying.

NUTRITIONAL INFO (approximate, per serving)

- Calories: 50-75 | Protein: 1-2g | Fat: 5-8g | Carbohydrates: 5-8g | Fiber: 1-2g | Net Carbs: 3-5g

Thai Peanut Stir-Fry Sauce

A flavorful and versatile sauce for your vegan stir-fries.

 **Yields:** About 1/4 cup

INGREDIENTS

- 1/4 cup creamy peanut butter

- 2 tablespoons soy sauce or tamari

- 1 tablespoon rice vinegar

- 1 tablespoon honey or maple syrup

- 1 tablespoon sesame oil

- 1 teaspoon minced garlic

- 1/4 teaspoon red pepper flakes

INSTRUCTIONS

1. In a small bowl, whisk together the peanut butter, soy sauce, rice vinegar, honey, sesame oil, garlic, and red pepper flakes.

2. Taste the sauce and adjust the ingredients to your liking. If it's too thick, add a little water to thin it out.

NOTES

- For a spicier sauce, add more red pepper flakes.

- To make this sauce gluten-free, use tamari instead of soy sauce.

- This sauce can be used to marinate tofu, tempeh, or vegetables before stir-frying.

NUTRITIONAL INFO (approximate, per serving)

- Calories: 150-200 | Protein: 3-5g | Fat: 15-20g | Carbohydrates: 10-15g | Fiber: 2-3g | Net Carbs: 8-12g

Maple Sriracha Stir-Fry Sauce

A sweet and spicy sauce for your vegan stir-fries.

 **Yields:** About 1/4 cup

INGREDIENTS

- 1/4 cup soy sauce or tamari

- 2 tablespoons rice vinegar

- 1 tablespoon maple syrup

- 1 tablespoon sriracha

- 1 teaspoon minced garlic

- 1/2 teaspoon red pepper flakes

INSTRUCTIONS

1. In a small bowl, whisk together the soy sauce, rice vinegar, maple syrup, sriracha, garlic, and red pepper flakes.

2. Taste the sauce and adjust the ingredients to your liking.

NOTES

- For a spicier sauce, add more sriracha or red pepper flakes.

- To make this sauce gluten-free, use tamari instead of soy sauce.

- This sauce can be used to marinate tofu, tempeh, or vegetables before stir-frying.

NUTRITIONAL INFO (approximate, per serving)

- Calories: 50-75 | Protein: 1-2g | Fat: 5-8g | Carbohydrates: 5-8g | Fiber: 1-2g | Net Carbs: 3-5g

Spicy Sesame Stir-Fry Sauce

A versatile sauce for any vegan stir-fry.

 **Yields:** About 1/4 cup

INGREDIENTS

- 1/4 cup soy sauce or tamari

- 2 tablespoons rice vinegar

- 1 tablespoon honey or maple syrup

- 1 tablespoon sesame oil

- 1 tablespoon chili oil

- 1 teaspoon minced garlic

- 1/2 teaspoon red pepper flakes

INSTRUCTIONS

1. In a small bowl, whisk together the soy sauce, rice vinegar, honey, sesame oil, chili oil, garlic, and red pepper flakes.

2. Taste the sauce and adjust the ingredients to your liking.

NOTES

- For a spicier sauce, add more chili oil or red pepper flakes.

- To make this sauce gluten-free, use tamari instead of soy sauce.

- This sauce can be used to marinate tofu, tempeh, or vegetables before stir-frying.

NUTRITIONAL INFO (approximate, per serving)

- Calories: 50-75 | Protein: 1-2g | Fat: 5-8g | Carbohydrates: 5-8g | Fiber: 1-2g | Net Carbs: 3-5g

VEGETABLE STIR FRY DISHES

Chiang Mai Noodles

A flavorful and satisfying vegan dish.

 **Prep Time:** 15 minutes || **Cook Time:** 10 minutes || **Yield:** 4 servings

INGREDIENTS

For the stir-fry:

- 1 tablespoon vegetable oil

- 1 onion, thinly sliced

- 2 cloves garlic, minced

- 1 inch piece ginger, grated

- 1/2 cup broccoli florets

- 1/2 cup carrots, thinly sliced

- 1/4 cup snow peas

- 1/4 cup red bell pepper, thinly sliced

- 8 ounces rice noodles (wide)

- 1/4 cup tamarind paste

- 1/4 cup water

- 2 tablespoons soy sauce or tamari

- 1 tablespoon rice vinegar

- 1 teaspoon honey or maple syrup

- 1/4 cup chopped peanuts

- 1/4 cup chopped scallions

INSTRUCTIONS

1. Cook the rice noodles. Drain and set aside.

2. Heat a wok or large skillet over high heat. Add the vegetable oil.

3. Add the onion, garlic, and ginger to the wok. Stir-fry for 1-2 minutes, or until fragrant.

4. Add the broccoli, carrots, snow peas, and red bell pepper to the wok. Stir-fry for 3-4 minutes, or until crisp-tender.

5. Add the cooked rice noodles to the wok. Break them apart with a spatula and stir-fry for 2-3 minutes, or until heated through.

6. Add the tamarind paste, water, soy sauce, rice vinegar, and honey to the wok. Stir-fry for 1 minute, or until the sauce is heated through.

7. Combine the vegetables, noodles, and sauce. Stir-fry for 1 minute more, or until everything is coated in the sauce. Sprinkle with chopped peanuts and scallions and serve immediately.

NOTES

- For a spicier dish, add red pepper flakes.

- To make this dish gluten-free, use tamari instead of soy sauce.

- Serve with a side of stir-fried vegetables or a salad for a complete meal.

NUTRITIONAL INFO (approximate, per serving)

- Calories: 350-400 | Protein: 15-20g | Fat: 15-20g | Carbohydrates: 30-35g | Fiber: 5-7g | Net Carbs: 25-30g

Hoisin Glazed Tofu and Mushroom Stir-Fry

A flavorful and savory vegan dish.

 **Prep Time:** 15 minutes ||  **Cook Time:** 10 minutes ||  **Yield:** 4 servings

INGREDIENTS

For the marinade:

- 1 block extra-firm tofu, pressed and cubed

- 1 tablespoon soy sauce or tamari

- 1 teaspoon rice vinegar

- 1/2 teaspoon cornstarch

- 1/4 teaspoon red pepper flakes

- 1/4 teaspoon garlic powder

- 1/4 teaspoon ginger powder

For the stir-fry:

- 1 tablespoon vegetable oil

- 1 onion, thinly sliced

- 2 cloves garlic, minced

- 1 inch piece ginger, grated

- 8 ounces mixed mushrooms (shiitake, cremini, oyster)

- 1/4 cup hoisin sauce

- 1 tablespoon rice vinegar

- 1 teaspoon honey or maple syrup

- 1/4 cup chopped scallions

INSTRUCTIONS

1. In a bowl, combine the tofu cubes with the marinade ingredients. Toss to coat and let marinate for at least 15 minutes, or up to 30 minutes.

2. Heat a wok or large skillet over high heat. Add the vegetable oil.

3. Add the onion, garlic, and ginger to the wok. Stir-fry for 1-2 minutes, or until fragrant.

4. Add the mixed mushrooms to the wok. Stir-fry for 3-4 minutes, or until cooked through and slightly browned.

5. Add the marinated tofu to the wok. Stir-fry for 3-4 minutes, or until browned and heated through.

6. Add the hoisin sauce, rice vinegar, and honey to the wok. Stir-fry for 1 minute, or until the sauce is heated through.

7. Combine the mushrooms and tofu with the sauce. Stir-fry for 1 minute more, or until everything is coated in the sauce. Sprinkle with chopped scallions and serve immediately over rice.

NOTES

- For a spicier dish, add red pepper flakes.

- To make this dish gluten-free, use tamari instead of soy sauce.

- Serve over brown rice or cauliflower rice for a complete meal.

NUTRITIONAL INFO (approximate, per serving)

- Calories: 300-350 | Protein: 20-25g | Fat: 15-20g | Carbohydrates: 20-25g | Fiber: 5-7g | Net Carbs: 15-18g

Mongolian Vegetable and Seitan Stir-Fry

A flavorful and satisfying vegan dish.

 **Prep Time:** 15 minutes || **Cook Time:** 10 minutes || **Yield:** 4 servings

INGREDIENTS

For the marinade:

- 1 block extra-firm tofu, pressed and cubed

- 1 tablespoon soy sauce or tamari

- 1 teaspoon rice vinegar

- 1/2 teaspoon cornstarch

- 1/4 teaspoon red pepper flakes

- 1/4 teaspoon garlic powder

- 1/4 teaspoon ginger powder

For the stir-fry:

- 1 tablespoon vegetable oil

- 1 onion, thinly sliced

- 2 cloves garlic, minced

- 1 inch piece ginger, grated

- 1/2 cup broccoli florets

- 1/2 cup carrots, thinly sliced

- 1/4 cup snow peas

- 1/4 cup red bell pepper, thinly sliced

- 1/4 cup vegetable broth

- 2 tablespoons Mongolian barbecue sauce

- 1 tablespoon rice vinegar

- 1 teaspoon honey or maple syrup

INSTRUCTIONS

1. In a bowl, combine the tofu cubes with the marinade ingredients. Toss to coat and let marinate for at least 15 minutes, or up to 30 minutes.

2. Heat a wok or large skillet over high heat. Add the vegetable oil.

3. Add the onion, garlic, and ginger to the wok. Stir-fry for 1-2 minutes, or until fragrant.

4. Add the broccoli, carrots, snow peas, and red bell pepper to the wok. Stir-fry for 3-4 minutes, or until crisp-tender.

5. Add the marinated tofu to the wok. Stir-fry for 3-4 minutes, or until browned and heated through.

6. Add the vegetable broth, Mongolian barbecue sauce, rice vinegar, and honey to the wok. Stir-fry for 1 minute, or until the sauce is heated through.

7. Combine the vegetables and tofu with the sauce. Stir-fry for 1 minute more, or until everything is coated in the sauce. Serve immediately over rice.

NOTES

- For a spicier dish, add more red pepper flakes.

- To make this dish gluten-free, use tamari instead of soy sauce.

- Serve over brown rice or cauliflower rice for a complete meal.

NUTRITIONAL INFO (approximate, per serving)

- Calories: 300-350 | Protein: 20-25g | Fat: 15-20g | Carbohydrates: 20-25g | Fiber: 5-7g | Net Carbs: 15-18g

Spicy Thai Pineapple Stir-Fry

A flavorful and aromatic vegan dish.

**Prep Time:** 15 minutes || **Cook Time:** 10 minutes || **Yield:** 4 servings

INGREDIENTS

For the stir-fry:

- 1 tablespoon vegetable oil

- 1 onion, thinly sliced

- 2 cloves garlic, minced

- 1 inch piece ginger, grated

- 1 can (14.5 oz) pineapple chunks, drained

- 1 red bell pepper, thinly sliced

- 1/4 cup vegetable broth

- 2 tablespoons soy sauce or tamari

- 1 tablespoon rice vinegar

- 1 teaspoon honey or maple syrup

- 1/2 teaspoon red pepper flakes

- 1/4 cup chopped fresh basil

INSTRUCTIONS

1. Heat a wok or large skillet over high heat. Add the vegetable oil.

2. Add the onion, garlic, and ginger to the wok. Stir-fry for 1-2 minutes, or until fragrant.

3. Add the pineapple chunks and red bell pepper to the wok. Stir-fry for 2-3 minutes, or until crisp-tender.

4. Add the vegetable broth, soy sauce, rice vinegar, honey, and red pepper flakes to the wok. Stir-fry for 1 minute, or until the sauce is heated through.

5. Combine the pineapple, bell pepper, and sauce. Stir-fry for 1 minute more, or until everything is coated in the sauce. Sprinkle with chopped basil and serve immediately over rice.

NOTES

- To make this dish gluten-free, use tamari instead of soy sauce.

- Serve over brown rice or cauliflower rice for a complete meal.

NUTRITIONAL INFO (approximate, per serving)

- Calories: 300-350 | Protein: 15-20g | Fat: 15-20g | Carbohydrates: 20-25g | Fiber: 5-7g | Net Carbs: 15-18g

Sweet and Sour Chickpea Stir-Fry

A flavorful and tangy vegan dish.

 **Prep Time:** 15 minutes || **Cook Time:** 10 minutes || **Yield:** 4 servings

INGREDIENTS

For the stir-fry:

- 1 tablespoon vegetable oil

- 1 onion, thinly sliced

- 2 cloves garlic, minced

- 1 inch piece ginger, grated

- 1 can (15 ounces) chickpeas, drained and rinsed

- 1 red bell pepper, thinly sliced

- 1/4 cup vegetable broth

- 1/4 cup sweet and sour sauce

- 1 tablespoon soy sauce or tamari

- 1 tablespoon rice vinegar

- 1 teaspoon honey or maple syrup

INSTRUCTIONS

1. Heat a wok or large skillet over high heat. Add the vegetable oil.

2. Add the onion, garlic, and ginger to the wok. Stir-fry for 1-2 minutes, or until fragrant.

3. Add the chickpeas and red bell pepper to the wok. Stir-fry for 3-4 minutes, or until heated through.

4. In a small bowl, whisk together the vegetable broth, sweet and sour sauce, soy sauce, rice vinegar, and honey.

5. Pour the sauce over the vegetables and chickpeas. Stir-fry for 1 minute more, or until everything is coated in the sauce. Serve immediately over rice.

NOTES

- To make this dish gluten-free, use tamari instead of soy sauce.

- Serve over brown rice or cauliflower rice for a complete meal.

NUTRITIONAL INFO (approximate, per serving)

- Calories: 300-350 | Protein: 20-25g | Fat: 10-15g | Carbohydrates: 20-25g | Fiber: 5-7g | Net Carbs: 15-18g

Coconut Curry Vegetable Stir-Fry

A flavorful and aromatic vegan dish.

 **Prep Time:** 15 minutes || **Cook Time:** 10 minutes || **Yield:** 4 servings

INGREDIENTS

For the stir-fry:

- 1 tablespoon vegetable oil
- 1 onion, thinly sliced
- 2 cloves garlic, minced
- 1 inch piece ginger, grated
- 1 cup broccoli florets
- 1/2 cup carrots, thinly sliced
- 1/4 cup snow peas
- 1/4 cup red bell pepper, thinly sliced
- 1/4 cup coconut milk
- 2 tablespoons curry powder
- 1 tablespoon soy sauce or tamari
- 1 teaspoon rice vinegar
- 1 teaspoon honey or maple syrup

INSTRUCTIONS

1. Heat a wok or large skillet over high heat. Add the vegetable oil.

2. Add the onion, garlic, and ginger to the wok. Stir-fry for 1-2 minutes, or until fragrant.

3. Add the broccoli, carrots, snow peas, and red bell pepper to the wok. Stir-fry for 3-4 minutes, or until crisp-tender.

4. Add the coconut milk, curry powder, soy sauce, rice vinegar, and honey to the wok. Stir-fry for 1 minute, or until the sauce is heated through.

5. Combine the vegetables with the sauce. Stir-fry for 1 minute more, or until everything is coated in the sauce. Serve immediately over rice.

NOTES

- To make this dish gluten-free, use tamari instead of soy sauce.

- Serve over brown rice or cauliflower rice for a complete meal.

NUTRITIONAL INFO (approximate, per serving)

- Calories: 350-400 | Protein: 15-20g | Fat: 20-25g | Carbohydrates: 20-25g | Fiber: 5-7g | Net Carbs: 15-18g

Lemon Garlic Broccoli Stir-Fry

A quick and flavorful vegan dish.

 **Prep Time:** 15 minutes || **Cook Time:** 10 minutes || **Yield:** 4 servings

INGREDIENTS

For the stir-fry:

- 1 tablespoon vegetable oil

- 1 onion, thinly sliced

- 2 cloves garlic, minced

- 1 inch piece ginger, grated

- 1 head broccoli, cut into florets

- 1/4 cup vegetable broth

- 2 tablespoons soy sauce or tamari

- 1 tablespoon rice vinegar

- 1 teaspoon honey or maple syrup

- 1 tablespoon lemon juice

- 1/4 teaspoon red pepper flakes (optional)

INSTRUCTIONS

1. Heat a wok or large skillet over high heat. Add the vegetable oil.

2. Add the onion, garlic, and ginger to the wok. Stir-fry for 1-2 minutes, or until fragrant.

3. Add the broccoli florets to the wok. Stir-fry for 3-4 minutes, or until crisp-tender.

4. In a small bowl, whisk together the vegetable broth, soy sauce, rice vinegar, honey, lemon juice, and red pepper flakes (if using).

5. Pour the sauce over the broccoli. Stir-fry for 1 minute more, or until everything is coated in the sauce. Serve immediately over rice.

NOTES

- For a spicier dish, add more red pepper flakes.

- To make this dish gluten-free, use tamari instead of soy sauce.

- Serve over brown rice or cauliflower rice for a complete meal.

NUTRITIONAL INFO (approximate, per serving)

- Calories: 250-300 | Protein: 10-15g | Fat: 10-15g | Carbohydrates: 20-25g | Fiber: 5-7g | Net Carbs: 15-18g

Spicy Chinese Curry Tempeh Stir-Fry

A flavorful and hearty vegan dish.

 **Prep Time:** 15 minutes || **Cook Time:** 10 minutes || **Yield:** 4 servings

INGREDIENTS

For the marinade:

- 1 block extra-firm tofu, pressed and cubed

- 1 tablespoon soy sauce or tamari

- 1 teaspoon rice vinegar

- 1/2 teaspoon cornstarch

- 1/4 teaspoon red pepper flakes

- 1/4 teaspoon garlic powder

- 1/4 teaspoon ginger powder

For the stir-fry:

- 1 tablespoon vegetable oil

- 1 onion, thinly sliced

- 2 cloves garlic, minced

- 1 inch piece ginger, grated

- 1 red bell pepper, thinly sliced

- 1/4 cup curry paste

- 1/4 cup vegetable broth

- 2 tablespoons soy sauce or tamari

- 1 tablespoon rice vinegar

- 1 teaspoon honey or maple syrup

INSTRUCTIONS

1. In a bowl, combine the tofu cubes with the marinade ingredients. Toss to coat and let marinate for at least 15 minutes, or up to 30 minutes.

2. Heat a wok or large skillet over high heat. Add the vegetable oil.

3. Add the onion, garlic, and ginger to the wok. Stir-fry for 1-2 minutes, or until fragrant.

4. Add the red bell pepper to the wok. Stir-fry for 2-3 minutes, or until crisp-tender.

5. Add the marinated tofu to the wok. Stir-fry for 3-4 minutes, or until browned and heated through.

6. Add the curry paste, vegetable broth, soy sauce, rice vinegar, and honey to the wok. Stir-fry for 1 minute, or until the sauce is heated through.

7. Combine the vegetables, tempeh, and sauce. Stir-fry for 1 minute more, or until everything is coated in the sauce. Serve immediately over rice.

NOTES

- For a spicier dish, add more red pepper flakes or use a spicier curry paste.

- To make this dish gluten-free, use tamari instead of soy sauce.

- Serve over brown rice or cauliflower rice for a complete meal.

NUTRITIONAL INFO (approximate, per serving)

- Calories: 300-350 | Protein: 20-25g | Fat: 15-20g | Carbohydrates: 20-25g | Fiber: 5-7g | Net Carbs: 15-18g

General Tso's Cauliflower Stir-Fry

A flavorful and spicy vegan dish.

 **Prep Time:** 15 minutes || **Cook Time:** 10 minutes || **Yield:** 4 servings

INGREDIENTS

For the cauliflower:

- 1 head cauliflower, cut into florets

- 1/4 cup cornstarch

- 1/4 teaspoon salt

- 1/4 teaspoon black pepper

For the sauce:

- 1/4 cup soy sauce or tamari

- 2 tablespoons rice vinegar

- 1 tablespoon honey or maple syrup

- 1 tablespoon chili oil

- 1 teaspoon garlic powder

- 1/2 teaspoon ginger powder

- 1/4 cup vegetable broth

For the stir-fry:

- 1 tablespoon vegetable oil

- 1 onion, thinly sliced

- 2 cloves garlic, minced

- 1 inch piece ginger, grated

- 1/4 cup chopped scallions

INSTRUCTIONS

1. In a bowl, combine the cauliflower florets with the cornstarch, salt, and pepper. Toss to coat.

2. In a small bowl, whisk together the soy sauce, rice vinegar, honey, chili oil, garlic powder, ginger powder, and vegetable broth.

3. Heat a wok or large skillet over high heat. Add the vegetable oil.

4. Add the onion, garlic, and ginger to the wok. Stir-fry for 1-2 minutes, or until fragrant.

5. Add the coated cauliflower florets to the wok. Stir-fry for 3-4 minutes, or until crisp-tender and lightly browned.

6. Pour the sauce over the cauliflower. Stir-fry for 1 minute more, or until the cauliflower is coated in the sauce. Serve immediately, garnished with chopped scallions.

NOTES

- For a spicier dish, add more chili oil or red pepper flakes.

- To make this dish gluten-free, use tamari instead of soy sauce.

- Serve over rice or noodles for a complete meal.

NUTRITIONAL INFO (approximate, per serving)

- Calories: 250-300 | Protein: 10-15g | Fat: 10-15g | Carbohydrates: 20-25g | Fiber: 5-7g | Net Carbs: 15-18g

Mushroom and Bok Choy Stir-Fry

A quick and flavorful vegan dish.

 **Prep Time:** 15 minutes || **Cook Time:** 10 minutes || **Yield:** 4 servings

INGREDIENTS

For the stir-fry:

- 1 tablespoon vegetable oil

- 1 onion, thinly sliced

- 2 cloves garlic, minced

- 1 inch piece ginger, grated

- 1 bunch bok choy, cut into wedges

- 8 ounces mixed mushrooms (shiitake, cremini, oyster)

- 1/4 cup vegetable broth

- 2 tablespoons soy sauce or tamari

- 1 tablespoon rice vinegar

- 1 teaspoon honey or maple syrup

INSTRUCTIONS

1. Heat a wok or large skillet over high heat. Add the vegetable oil.

2. Add the onion, garlic, and ginger to the wok. Stir-fry for 1-2 minutes, or until fragrant.

3. Add the bok choy and mushrooms to the wok. Stir-fry for 3-4 minutes, or until crisp-tender.

4. Add the vegetable broth, soy sauce, rice vinegar, and honey to the wok. Stir-fry for 1 minute, or until the sauce is heated through.

5. Combine the vegetables with the sauce. Stir-fry for 1 minute more, or until everything is coated in the sauce. Serve immediately over rice.

NOTES

- For a spicier dish, add red pepper flakes.

- To make this dish gluten-free, use tamari instead of soy sauce.

- Serve over brown rice or cauliflower rice for a complete meal.

NUTRITIONAL INFO (approximate, per serving)

- Calories: 250-300 | Protein: 10-15g | Fat: 15-20g | Carbohydrates: 20-25g | Fiber: 5-7g | Net Carbs: 15-18g

Blood Orange Broccoli Stir-Fry

A tangy and flavorful vegan dish.

 **Prep Time:** 15 minutes || **Cook Time:** 10 minutes || **Yield:** 4 servings

INGREDIENTS

For the stir-fry:

- 1 tablespoon vegetable oil

- 1 onion, thinly sliced

- 2 cloves garlic, minced

- 1 inch piece ginger, grated

- 1 head broccoli, cut into florets

- 1/2 cup blood orange juice

- 1/4 cup orange zest

- 2 tablespoons soy sauce or tamari

- 1 tablespoon rice vinegar

- 1 teaspoon honey or maple syrup

- 1/2 teaspoon red pepper flakes

INSTRUCTIONS

1. Heat a wok or large skillet over high heat. Add the vegetable oil.

2. Add the onion, garlic, and ginger to the wok. Stir-fry for 1-2 minutes, or until fragrant.

3. Add the broccoli florets to the wok. Stir-fry for 3-4 minutes, or until crisp-tender.

4. In a small bowl, whisk together the blood orange juice, orange zest, soy sauce, rice vinegar, honey, and red pepper flakes.

5. Pour the sauce over the broccoli. Stir-fry for 1 minute more, or until everything is coated in the sauce. Serve immediately over rice.

NOTES

- For a spicier dish, add more red pepper flakes.

- To make this dish gluten-free, use tamari instead of soy sauce.

- Serve over brown rice or cauliflower rice for a complete meal.

NUTRITIONAL INFO (approximate, per serving)

- Calories: 250-300 | Protein: 10-15g | Fat: 10-15g | Carbohydrates: 20-25g | Fiber: 5-7g | Net Carbs: 15-18g

Curried Millet and Kohlrabi Stir-Fry

A flavorful and nutritious vegan dish.

 **Prep Time:** 15 minutes || **Cook Time:** 15 minutes || **Yield:** 4 servings

INGREDIENTS

For the stir-fry:

- 1 tablespoon vegetable oil

- 1 onion, thinly sliced

- 2 cloves garlic, minced

- 1 inch piece ginger, grated

- 1 cup cooked millet

- 1 kohlrabi, cubed

- 1/4 cup snow peas

- 1/4 cup red bell pepper, thinly sliced

- 1/4 cup vegetable broth

- 2 tablespoons curry powder

- 1 tablespoon soy sauce or tamari

- 1 tablespoon rice vinegar

- 1 teaspoon honey or maple syrup

INSTRUCTIONS

1. Heat a wok or large skillet over high heat. Add the vegetable oil.

2. Add the onion, garlic, and ginger to the wok. Stir-fry for 1-2 minutes, or until fragrant.

3. Add the kohlrabi, snow peas, and red bell pepper to the wok. Stir-fry for 3-4 minutes, or until crisp-tender.

4. Add the cooked millet to the wok. Break it apart with a spatula and stir-fry for 2-3 minutes, or until heated through.

5. Add the vegetable broth, soy sauce, rice vinegar, honey, and curry powder to the wok. Stir-fry for 1 minute, or until the sauce is heated through.

6. Combine the vegetables, millet, and sauce. Stir-fry for 1 minute more, or until everything is coated in the sauce. Serve immediately.

NOTES

- For a spicier dish, add red pepper flakes.

- To make this dish gluten-free, use tamari instead of soy sauce.

- Serve with a side of stir-fried vegetables or a salad for a complete meal.

NUTRITIONAL INFO (approximate, per serving)

- Calories: 350-400 | Protein: 15-20g | Fat: 15-20g | Carbohydrates: 30-35g | Fiber: 5-7g | Net Carbs: 25-30g

Peanut Sauce Vegetable Stir-Fry with Cauliflower Rice

A flavorful and satisfying vegan dish.

 **Prep Time:** 15 minutes || **Cook Time:** 10 minutes || **Yield:** 4 servings

INGREDIENTS

For the stir-fry:

- 1 tablespoon vegetable oil

- 1 onion, thinly sliced

- 2 cloves garlic, minced

- 1 inch piece ginger, grated

- 1 cup broccoli florets

- 1/2 cup carrots, thinly sliced

- 1/4 cup snow peas

- 1 cup cooked cauliflower rice

- 1/4 cup peanut butter

- 1/4 cup soy sauce or tamari

- 1 tablespoon rice vinegar

- 1 tablespoon honey or maple syrup

- 1 tablespoon sesame oil

- 1/4 cup chopped peanuts

INSTRUCTIONS

1. Heat a wok or large skillet over high heat. Add the vegetable oil.

2. Add the onion, garlic, and ginger to the wok. Stir-fry for 1-2 minutes, or until fragrant.

3. Add the broccoli, carrots, and snow peas to the wok. Stir-fry for 3-4 minutes, or until crisp-tender.

4. Add the cooked cauliflower rice to the wok. Stir-fry for 2-3 minutes, or until heated through.

5. In a small bowl, whisk together the peanut butter, soy sauce, rice vinegar, honey, and sesame oil.

6. Pour the sauce over the stir-fried vegetables and cauliflower rice. Toss to coat. Sprinkle with chopped peanuts and serve immediately.

NOTES

- For a spicier dish, add red pepper flakes to the sauce.

- To make this dish gluten-free, use tamari instead of soy sauce.

- Serve with a side of steamed vegetables or a salad.

NUTRITIONAL INFO (approximate, per serving)

- Calories: 350-400 | Protein: 20-25g | Fat: 20-25g | Carbohydrates: 20-25g | Fiber: 5-7g | Net Carbs: 15-18g

Okra and Cherry Tomato Stir-Fry

A quick and flavorful vegan dish.

 **Prep Time:** 15 minutes || **Cook Time:** 10 minutes || **Yield:** 4 servings

INGREDIENTS

For the stir-fry:

- 1 tablespoon vegetable oil

- 1 onion, thinly sliced

- 2 cloves garlic, minced

- 1 inch piece ginger, grated

- 1 pound okra, sliced

- 1 pint cherry tomatoes, halved

- 1/4 cup vegetable broth

- 2 tablespoons soy sauce or tamari

- 1 tablespoon rice vinegar

- 1 teaspoon honey or maple syrup

INSTRUCTIONS

1. Heat a wok or large skillet over high heat. Add the vegetable oil.

2. Add the onion, garlic, and ginger to the wok. Stir-fry for 1-2 minutes, or until fragrant.

3. Add the sliced okra and cherry tomatoes to the wok. Stir-fry for 3-4 minutes, or until the okra is tender-crisp and the tomatoes burst open.

4. Add the vegetable broth, soy sauce, rice vinegar, and honey to the wok. Stir-fry for 1 minute, or until the sauce is heated through.

5. Combine the vegetables with the sauce. Stir-fry for 1 minute more, or until everything is coated in the sauce. Serve immediately over rice.

NOTES

- For a spicier dish, add red pepper flakes.

- To make this dish gluten-free, use tamari instead of soy sauce.

- Serve over brown rice or cauliflower rice for a complete meal.

NUTRITIONAL INFO (approximate, per serving)

- Calories: 250-300 | Protein: 10-15g | Fat: 10-15g | Carbohydrates: 20-25g | Fiber: 5-7g | Net Carbs: 15-18g

Black Bean Noodle Stir-Fry with Orange Sauce

A flavorful and tangy vegan dish.

 **Prep Time:** 15 minutes || **Cook Time:** 10 minutes || **Yield:** 4 servings

INGREDIENTS

For the stir-fry:

- 1 tablespoon vegetable oil

- 1 onion, thinly sliced

- 2 cloves garlic, minced

- 1 inch piece ginger, grated

- 1/2 cup black bean sauce

- 1/4 cup orange juice

- 1/4 cup orange zest

- 2 tablespoons soy sauce or tamari

- 1 tablespoon rice vinegar

- 1 teaspoon honey or maple syrup

- 1/2 teaspoon red pepper flakes

- 8 ounces rice noodles, cooked according to package instructions

INSTRUCTIONS

1. Cook the rice noodles. Drain and set aside.

2. Heat a wok or large skillet over high heat. Add the vegetable oil.

3. Add the onion, garlic, and ginger to the wok. Stir-fry for 1-2 minutes, or until fragrant.

4. Add the black bean sauce, orange juice, orange zest, soy sauce, rice vinegar, honey, and red pepper flakes to the wok. Stir-fry for 1 minute, or until the sauce is heated through.

5. Add the cooked rice noodles to the wok. Break them apart with a spatula and stir-fry for 2-3 minutes, or until coated in the sauce. Serve immediately, garnished with chopped scallions.

NOTES

- For a spicier dish, add more red pepper flakes.

- To make this dish gluten-free, use tamari instead of soy sauce.

- Serve with a side of stir-fried vegetables or a salad for a complete meal.

NUTRITIONAL INFO (approximate, per serving)

- Calories: 350-400 | Protein: 20-25g | Fat: 15-20g | Carbohydrates: 30-35g | Fiber: 5-7g | Net Carbs: 25-30g

Lotus Root and Green Onion Stir-Fry

A refreshing and flavorful vegan dish.

 **Prep Time:** 15 minutes || **Cook Time:** 10 minutes || **Yield:** 4 servings

INGREDIENTS

For the stir-fry:

- 1 tablespoon vegetable oil

- 1 onion, thinly sliced

- 2 cloves garlic, minced

- 1 inch piece ginger, grated

- 1 lotus root, sliced into thin rounds

- 1 bunch green onions, thinly sliced

- 1/4 cup vegetable broth

- 2 tablespoons soy sauce or tamari

- 1 tablespoon rice vinegar

- 1 teaspoon honey or maple syrup

INSTRUCTIONS

1. Peel the lotus root and slice it into thin rounds. Soak in cold water for 10-15 minutes to remove any bitterness. Drain and pat dry.

2. Heat a wok or large skillet over high heat. Add the vegetable oil.

3. Add the onion, garlic, and ginger to the wok. Stir-fry for 1-2 minutes, or until fragrant.

4. Add the lotus root and green onions to the wok. Stir-fry for 3-4 minutes, or until crisp-tender.

5. Add the vegetable broth, soy sauce, rice vinegar, and honey to the wok. Stir-fry for 1 minute, or until the sauce is heated through.

6. Combine the vegetables with the sauce. Stir-fry for 1 minute more, or until everything is coated in the sauce. Serve immediately over rice.

NOTES

- To make this dish gluten-free, use tamari instead of soy sauce.

- Serve over brown rice or cauliflower rice for a complete meal.

NUTRITIONAL INFO (approximate, per serving)

- Calories: 250-300 | Protein: 10-15g | Fat: 10-15g | Carbohydrates: 20-25g | Fiber: 5-7g | Net Carbs: 15-18g

Zucchini Noodle Stir-Fry

A light and healthy vegan dish.

Prep Time: 15 minutes || **Cook Time:** 10 minutes || **Yield:** 4 servings

INGREDIENTS

For the stir-fry:

- 1 tablespoon vegetable oil

- 1 onion, thinly sliced

- 2 cloves garlic, minced

- 1 inch piece ginger, grated

- 2 large zucchini, spiralized into noodles

- 1/4 cup snap peas

- 1/4 cup red bell pepper, thinly sliced

- 1/4 cup vegetable broth

- 2 tablespoons soy sauce or tamari

- 1 tablespoon rice vinegar

- 1 teaspoon honey or maple syrup

INSTRUCTIONS

1. Heat a wok or large skillet over high heat. Add the vegetable oil.

2. Add the onion, garlic, and ginger to the wok. Stir-fry for 1-2 minutes, or until fragrant.

3. Add the zucchini noodles, snap peas, and red bell pepper to the wok. Stir-fry for 3-4 minutes, or until crisp-tender.

4. Add the vegetable broth, soy sauce, rice vinegar, and honey to the wok. Stir-fry for 1 minute, or until the sauce is heated through.

5. Combine the vegetables with the sauce. Stir-fry for 1 minute more, or until everything is coated in the sauce. Serve immediately.

NOTES

- For a spicier dish, add red pepper flakes.

- To make this dish gluten-free, use tamari instead of soy sauce.

- Serve with a side of stir-fried vegetables or a salad for a complete meal.

NUTRITIONAL INFO (approximate, per serving)

- Calories: 250-300 | Protein: 10-15g | Fat: 10-15g | Carbohydrates: 20-25g | Fiber: 5-7g | Net Carbs: 15-18g

Broccoli and Red Pepper Tofu Stir-Fry

A quick and easy vegan dish.

 **Prep Time:** 15 minutes || **Cook Time:** 10 minutes || **Yield:** 4 servings

INGREDIENTS

For the marinade:

- 1 block extra-firm tofu, pressed and cubed

- 1 tablespoon soy sauce or tamari

- 1 teaspoon rice vinegar

- 1/2 teaspoon cornstarch

- 1/4 teaspoon red pepper flakes

- 1/4 teaspoon garlic powder

- 1/4 teaspoon ginger powder

For the stir-fry:

- 1 tablespoon vegetable oil

- 1 onion, thinly sliced

- 2 cloves garlic, minced

- 1 inch piece ginger, grated

- 1 head broccoli, cut into florets

- 1 red bell pepper, thinly sliced

- 1/4 cup vegetable broth

- 2 tablespoons soy sauce or tamari

- 1 tablespoon rice vinegar

- 1 teaspoon honey or maple syrup

INSTRUCTIONS

1. In a bowl, combine the tofu cubes with the marinade ingredients. Toss to coat and let marinate for at least 15 minutes, or up to 30 minutes.

2. Heat a wok or large skillet over high heat. Add the vegetable oil.

3. Add the onion, garlic, and ginger to the wok. Stir-fry for 1-2 minutes, or until fragrant.

4. Add the broccoli and red bell pepper to the wok. Stir-fry for 3-4 minutes, or until crisp-tender.

5. Add the marinated tofu to the wok. Stir-fry for 3-4 minutes, or until browned and heated through.

6. Add the vegetable broth, soy sauce, rice vinegar, and honey to the wok. Stir-fry for 1 minute, or until the sauce is heated through.

7. Combine the vegetables and tofu with the sauce. Stir-fry for 1 minute more, or until everything is coated in the sauce. Serve immediately over rice.

NOTES

- For a spicier dish, add more red pepper flakes.

- To make this dish gluten-free, use tamari instead of soy sauce.

- Serve over brown rice or cauliflower rice for a complete meal.

NUTRITIONAL INFO (approximate, per serving)

- Calories: 250-300 | Protein: 20-25g | Fat: 10-15g | Carbohydrates: 20-25g | Fiber: 5-7g | Net Carbs: 15-18g

Keerai Poriyal (Spinach Stir-Fry)

A classic South Indian side dish.

 **Prep Time:** 15 minutes || **Cook Time:** 10 minutes || **Yield:** 4 servings

INGREDIENTS

- 1 bunch spinach, chopped

- 1 tablespoon coconut oil

- 1/2 teaspoon mustard seeds

- 1 dry red chili, broken into pieces

- 1 pinch asafoetida powder

- 1/4 teaspoon turmeric powder

- 1/4 teaspoon salt

INSTRUCTIONS

1. In a wok or large skillet, heat the coconut oil over medium heat. Add the mustard seeds and let them sizzle until they start to pop.

2. Add the dry red chili, asafoetida powder, turmeric powder, and salt. Stir for a few seconds.

3. Add the chopped spinach to the wok. Stir-fry until the spinach wilts and the water has evaporated.

4. Serve hot as a side dish.

NOTES

- For a spicier dish, add more red chili or a pinch of cayenne pepper.

- You can substitute spinach with other leafy greens like kale, collard greens, or fenugreek leaves.

NUTRITIONAL INFO (approximate, per serving)

- Calories: 100-150 | Protein: 5-7g | Fat: 10-15g | Carbohydrates: 5-8g | Fiber: 2-3g | Net Carbs: 3-5g

Rainbow Vegetable Quinoa Stir-Fry

A vibrant and flavorful vegan dish.

 **Prep Time:** 15 minutes || **Cook Time:** 10 minutes || **Yield:** 4 servings

INGREDIENTS

For the stir-fry:

- 1 tablespoon vegetable oil

- 1 onion, thinly sliced

- 2 cloves garlic, minced

- 1 inch piece ginger, grated

- 1 cup cooked quinoa

- 1/2 cup carrots, thinly sliced

- 1/4 cup snow peas

- 1/4 cup red bell pepper, thinly sliced

- 1/4 cup yellow bell pepper, thinly sliced

- 1/4 cup green bell pepper, thinly sliced

- 1/4 cup broccoli florets

- 1/4 cup snap peas

- 1/4 cup vegetable broth

- 2 tablespoons soy sauce or tamari

- 1 tablespoon rice vinegar

- 1 teaspoon honey or maple syrup

INSTRUCTIONS

1. Heat a wok or large skillet over high heat. Add the vegetable oil.

2. Add the onion, garlic, and ginger to the wok. Stir-fry for 1-2 minutes, or until fragrant.

3. Add the carrots, snow peas, red bell pepper, yellow bell pepper, green bell pepper, broccoli, and snap peas to the wok. Stir-fry for 3-4 minutes, or until crisp-tender.

4. Add the cooked quinoa to the wok. Break it apart with a spatula and stir-fry for 2-3 minutes, or until heated through.

5. Add the vegetable broth, soy sauce, rice vinegar, and honey to the wok. Stir-fry for 1 minute, or until the sauce is heated through.

6. Combine the vegetables, quinoa, and sauce. Stir-fry for 1 minute more, or until everything is coated in the sauce. Serve immediately.

NOTES

- For a spicier dish, add red pepper flakes.

- To make this dish gluten-free, use tamari instead of soy sauce.

- Serve with a side of stir-fried vegetables or a salad for a complete meal.

NUTRITIONAL INFO (approximate, per serving)

- Calories: 350-400 | Protein: 15-20g | Fat: 15-20g | Carbohydrates: 30-35g | Fiber: 5-7g | Net Carbs: 25-30g

Lean and Green Tofu Stir-Fry

A healthy and flavorful vegan dish.

 **Prep Time:** 15 minutes || **Cook Time:** 10 minutes || **Yield:** 4 servings

INGREDIENTS

For the marinade:

- 1 block extra-firm tofu, pressed and cubed

- 1 tablespoon soy sauce or tamari

- 1 teaspoon rice vinegar

- 1/2 teaspoon cornstarch

- 1/4 teaspoon red pepper flakes

- 1/4 teaspoon garlic powder

- 1/4 teaspoon ginger powder

For the stir-fry:

- 1 tablespoon vegetable oil

- 1 onion, thinly sliced

- 2 cloves garlic, minced

- 1 inch piece ginger, grated

- 1 cup broccoli florets

- 1/2 cup snow peas

- 1/4 cup green beans

- 1/4 cup carrots, thinly sliced

- 1/4 cup vegetable broth

- 2 tablespoons soy sauce or tamari

- 1 tablespoon rice vinegar

- 1 teaspoon honey or maple syrup

INSTRUCTIONS

1. In a bowl, combine the tofu cubes with the marinade ingredients. Toss to coat and let marinate for at least 15 minutes, or up to 30 minutes.

2. Heat a wok or large skillet over high heat. Add the vegetable oil.

3. Add the onion, garlic, and ginger to the wok. Stir-fry for 1-2 minutes, or until fragrant.

4. Add the broccoli, snow peas, green beans, and carrots to the wok. Stir-fry for 3-4 minutes, or until crisp-tender.

5. Add the marinated tofu to the wok. Stir-fry for 3-4 minutes, or until browned and heated through.

6. Add the vegetable broth, soy sauce, rice vinegar, and honey to the wok. Stir-fry for 1 minute, or until the sauce is heated through.

7. Combine the vegetables and tofu with the sauce. Stir-fry for 1 minute more, or until everything is coated in the sauce. Serve immediately over rice.

NOTES

- For a spicier dish, add more red pepper flakes.

- To make this dish gluten-free, use tamari instead of soy sauce.

- Serve over brown rice or cauliflower rice for a complete meal.

NUTRITIONAL INFO (approximate, per serving)

- Calories: 250-300 | Protein: 20-25g | Fat: 10-15g | Carbohydrates: 20-25g | Fiber: 5-7g | Net Carbs: 15-18g

Tamarind Glazed Tempeh Stir-Fry

A tangy and flavorful vegan dish.

 **Prep Time:** 15 minutes || **Cook Time:** 10 minutes || **Yield:** 4 servings

INGREDIENTS

For the marinade:

- 1 block tempeh, pressed and crumbled

- 1 tablespoon soy sauce or tamari

- 1 teaspoon rice vinegar

- 1/2 teaspoon cornstarch

- 1/4 teaspoon red pepper flakes

- 1/4 teaspoon garlic powder

- 1/4 teaspoon ginger powder

For the stir-fry:

- 1 tablespoon vegetable oil

- 1 onion, thinly sliced

- 2 cloves garlic, minced

- 1 inch piece ginger, grated

- 1 red bell pepper, thinly sliced

- 1/4 cup tamarind paste

- 1/4 cup water

- 2 tablespoons soy sauce or tamari

- 1 tablespoon rice vinegar

- 1 teaspoon honey or maple syrup

INSTRUCTIONS

1. In a bowl, combine the tempeh with the marinade ingredients. Toss to coat and let marinate for at least 15 minutes, or up to 30 minutes.

2. Heat a wok or large skillet over high heat. Add the vegetable oil.

3. Add the onion, garlic, and ginger to the wok. Stir-fry for 1-2 minutes, or until fragrant.

4. Add the bell pepper to the wok. Stir-fry for 2-3 minutes, or until crisp-tender.

5. Add the marinated tempeh to the wok. Stir-fry for 3-4 minutes, or until browned and heated through.

6. Add the tamarind paste, water, soy sauce, rice vinegar, and honey to the wok. Stir-fry for 1 minute, or until the sauce is heated through.

7. Combine the vegetables and tempeh with the sauce. Stir-fry for 1 minute more, or until everything is coated in the sauce. Serve immediately over rice.

NOTES

- For a spicier dish, add more red pepper flakes.

- To make this dish gluten-free, use tamari instead of soy sauce.

- Serve over brown rice or cauliflower rice for a complete meal.

NUTRITIONAL INFO (approximate, per serving)

- Calories: 300-350 | Protein: 20-25g | Fat: 15-20g | Carbohydrates: 20-25g | Fiber: 5-7g | Net Carbs: 15-18g

Spicy Lentil Bulgur Stir-Fry

A hearty and flavorful vegan dish.

 **Prep Time:** 15 minutes || **Cook Time:** 15 minutes || **Yield:** 4 servings

INGREDIENTS

For the stir-fry:

- 1 tablespoon vegetable oil

- 1 onion, thinly sliced

- 2 cloves garlic, minced

- 1 inch piece ginger, grated

- 1 cup cooked brown lentils

- 1 cup cooked bulgur wheat

- 1/2 cup green peas

- 1/4 cup snow peas

- 1/4 cup red bell pepper, thinly sliced

- 1/4 cup vegetable broth

- 2 tablespoons soy sauce or tamari

- 1 tablespoon rice vinegar

- 1 teaspoon honey or maple syrup

- 1/2 teaspoon red pepper flakes

INSTRUCTIONS

1. Heat a wok or large skillet over high heat. Add the vegetable oil.

2. Add the onion, garlic, and ginger to the wok. Stir-fry for 1-2 minutes, or until fragrant.

3. Add the green peas, snow peas, and red bell pepper to the wok. Stir-fry for 3-4 minutes, or until crisp-tender.

4. Add the cooked lentils and bulgur wheat to the wok. Break apart with a spatula and stir-fry for 2-3 minutes, or until heated through.

5. Add the vegetable broth, soy sauce, rice vinegar, honey, and red pepper flakes to the wok. Stir-fry for 1 minute, or until the sauce is heated through.

6. Combine the vegetables, lentils, and bulgur with the sauce. Stir-fry for 1 minute more, or until everything is coated in the sauce. Serve immediately.

NOTES

- For a spicier dish, add more red pepper flakes.

- To make this dish gluten-free, use tamari instead of soy sauce.

- Serve with a side of stir-fried vegetables or a salad for a complete meal.

NUTRITIONAL INFO (approximate, per serving)

- Calories: 350-400 | Protein: 20-25g | Fat: 15-20g | Carbohydrates: 30-35g | Fiber: 5-7g | Net Carbs: 25-30g

Three Pea Ginger Tofu Stir-Fry

A flavorful and nutritious vegan dish.

 **Prep Time:** 15 minutes || **Cook Time:** 10 minutes || **Yield:** 4 servings

INGREDIENTS

For the marinade:

- 1 block extra-firm tofu, pressed and cubed

- 1 tablespoon soy sauce or tamari

- 1 teaspoon rice vinegar

- 1/2 teaspoon cornstarch

- 1/4 teaspoon red pepper flakes

- 1/4 teaspoon garlic powder

- 1/4 teaspoon ginger powder

For the stir-fry:

- 1 tablespoon vegetable oil

- 1 onion, thinly sliced

- 2 cloves garlic, minced

- 1 inch piece ginger, grated

- 1/2 cup snow peas

- 1/2 cup snap peas

- 1/4 cup English peas

- 1/4 cup vegetable broth

- 2 tablespoons soy sauce or tamari

- 1 tablespoon rice vinegar

- 1 teaspoon honey or maple syrup

INSTRUCTIONS

1. In a bowl, combine the tofu cubes with the marinade ingredients. Toss to coat and let marinate for at least 15 minutes, or up to 30 minutes.

2. Heat a wok or large skillet over high heat. Add the vegetable oil.

3. Add the onion, garlic, and ginger to the wok. Stir-fry for 1-2 minutes, or until fragrant.

4. Add the snow peas, snap peas, and English peas to the wok. Stir-fry for 3-4 minutes, or until crisp-tender.

5. Add the marinated tofu to the wok. Stir-fry for 3-4 minutes, or until browned and heated through.

6. Add the vegetable broth, soy sauce, rice vinegar, and honey to the wok. Stir-fry for 1 minute, or until the sauce is heated through.

7. Combine the peas and tofu with the sauce. Stir-fry for 1 minute more, or until everything is coated in the sauce. Serve immediately over rice.

NOTES

- For a spicier dish, add more red pepper flakes.

- To make this dish gluten-free, use tamari instead of soy sauce.

- Serve over brown rice or cauliflower rice for a complete meal.

NUTRITIONAL INFO (approximate, per serving)

- Calories: 250-300 | Protein: 20-25g | Fat: 10-15g | Carbohydrates: 20-25g | Fiber: 5-7g | Net Carbs: 15-18g

Tofu and Green Bean Stir-Fry

A quick and easy vegan dish.

 **Prep Time:** 15 minutes || **Cook Time:** 10 minutes || **Yield:** 4 servings

INGREDIENTS

For the marinade:

- 1 block extra-firm tofu, pressed and cubed

- 1 tablespoon soy sauce or tamari

- 1 teaspoon rice vinegar

- 1/2 teaspoon cornstarch

- 1/4 teaspoon red pepper flakes

- 1/4 teaspoon garlic powder

- 1/4 teaspoon ginger powder

- 1 tablespoon vegetable oil

- 1 onion, thinly sliced

- 2 cloves garlic, minced

- 1 inch piece ginger, grated

- 1 pound green beans, trimmed

- 1/4 cup vegetable broth

- 2 tablespoons soy sauce or tamari

- 1 tablespoon rice vinegar

- 1 teaspoon honey or maple syrup

For the stir-fry:

INSTRUCTIONS

1. In a bowl, combine the tofu cubes with the marinade ingredients. Toss to coat and let marinate for at least 15 minutes, or up to 30 minutes.

2. Heat a wok or large skillet over high heat. Add the vegetable oil.

3. Add the onion, garlic, and ginger to the wok. Stir-fry for 1-2 minutes, or until fragrant.

4. Add the green beans to the wok. Stir-fry for 3-4 minutes, or until crisp-tender.

5. Add the marinated tofu to the wok. Stir-fry for 3-4 minutes, or until browned and heated through.

6. Add the vegetable broth, soy sauce, rice vinegar, and honey to the wok. Stir-fry for 1 minute, or until the sauce is heated through.

7. Combine the green beans and tofu with the sauce. Stir-fry for 1 minute more, or until everything is coated in the sauce. Serve immediately over rice.

NOTES

- For a spicier dish, add more red pepper flakes.

- To make this dish gluten-free, use tamari instead of soy sauce.

- Serve over brown rice or cauliflower rice for a complete meal.

NUTRITIONAL INFO (approximate, per serving)

- Calories: 250-300 | Protein: 20-25g | Fat: 10-15g | Carbohydrates: 20-25g | Fiber: 5-7g | Net Carbs: 15-18g

Thai Basil Tempeh Stir-Fry

A flavorful and aromatic vegan dish.

 **Prep Time:** 15 minutes || **Cook Time:** 10 minutes || **Yield:** 4 servings

INGREDIENTS

For the marinade:

- 1 block tempeh, pressed and crumbled

- 1 tablespoon soy sauce or tamari

- 1 teaspoon rice vinegar

- 1/2 teaspoon cornstarch

- 1/4 teaspoon red pepper flakes

- 1/4 teaspoon garlic powder

- 1/4 teaspoon ginger powder

For the stir-fry:

- 1 tablespoon vegetable oil

- 1 onion, thinly sliced

- 2 cloves garlic, minced

- 1 inch piece ginger, grated

- 1 red bell pepper, thinly sliced

- 1 cup Thai basil leaves

- 1/4 cup vegetable broth

- 2 tablespoons soy sauce or tamari

- 1 tablespoon rice vinegar

- 1 teaspoon honey or maple syrup

- 1/2 teaspoon red pepper flakes

INSTRUCTIONS

1. In a bowl, combine the tempeh with the marinade ingredients. Toss to coat and let marinate for at least 15 minutes, or up to 30 minutes.

2. Heat a wok or large skillet over high heat. Add the vegetable oil.

3. Add the onion, garlic, and ginger to the wok. Stir-fry for 1-2 minutes, or until fragrant.

4. Add the bell pepper to the wok. Stir-fry for 2-3 minutes, or until crisp-tender.

5. Add the marinated tempeh to the wok. Stir-fry for 3-4 minutes, or until browned and heated through.

6. Add the vegetable broth, soy sauce, rice vinegar, honey, and red pepper flakes to the wok. Stir-fry for 1 minute, or until the sauce is heated through.

7. Add the Thai basil leaves to the wok. Stir-fry for 30 seconds, or until the basil is wilted but still retains its bright green color.

8. Serve immediately over rice.

NOTES

- For a spicier dish, add more red pepper flakes.

- To make this dish gluten-free, use tamari instead of soy sauce.

- Serve over brown rice or cauliflower rice for a complete meal.

NUTRITIONAL INFO (approximate, per serving)

- Calories: 300-350 | Protein: 20-25g | Fat: 15-20g | Carbohydrates: 20-25g | Fiber: 5-7g | Net Carbs: 15-18g

Spicy Szechuan Eggplant Stir-Fry

A flavorful and fiery vegan dish.

 **Prep Time:** 15 minutes || **Cook Time:** 10 minutes || **Yield:** 4 servings

INGREDIENTS

For the eggplant:

- 1 large eggplant, cubed

- 1 tablespoon cornstarch

- 1/4 teaspoon salt

For the Szechuan sauce:

- 1/4 cup soy sauce or tamari

- 1 tablespoon rice vinegar

- 1 tablespoon honey or maple syrup

- 1 teaspoon chili oil

- 1 teaspoon Sichuan peppercorns, ground

- 1/2 teaspoon red pepper flakes

- 1/4 teaspoon garlic powder

- 1/4 teaspoon ginger powder

For the stir-fry:

- 1 tablespoon vegetable oil

- 1 onion, thinly sliced

- 2 cloves garlic, minced

- 1 inch piece ginger, grated

- 1 red bell pepper, thinly sliced

INSTRUCTIONS

1. Toss the eggplant cubes with cornstarch and salt in a bowl. Set aside.

2. In a small bowl, whisk together the soy sauce, rice vinegar, honey, chili oil, Sichuan peppercorns, red pepper flakes, garlic powder, and ginger powder.

3. Heat a wok or large skillet over high heat. Add the vegetable oil.

4. Add the onion, garlic, and ginger to the wok. Stir-fry for 1-2 minutes, or until fragrant.

5. Add the prepared eggplant cubes to the wok. Stir-fry for 3-4 minutes, or until browned and cooked through.

6. Add the red bell pepper to the wok. Stir-fry for 2-3 minutes, or until crisp-tender.

7. Pour the Szechuan sauce over the vegetables. Stir-fry for 1 minute more, or until everything is coated in the sauce.

8. Serve immediately over rice.

NOTES

- For a spicier dish, add more chili oil, Sichuan peppercorns, or red pepper flakes.

- To make this dish gluten-free, use tamari instead of soy sauce.

- Serve over brown rice or cauliflower rice for a complete meal.

NUTRITIONAL INFO (approximate, per serving)

- Calories: 250-300 | Protein: 10-15g | Fat: 15-20g | Carbohydrates: 20-25g | Fiber: 5-7g | Net Carbs: 15-18g

Rainbow Pad Thai Stir-Fry

A vibrant and flavorful vegan dish.

 **Prep Time:** 15 minutes || **Cook Time:** 10 minutes || **Yield:** 4 servings

INGREDIENTS

For the stir-fry:

- 1 tablespoon vegetable oil

- 1 onion, thinly sliced

- 2 cloves garlic, minced

- 1 inch piece ginger, grated

- 1 cup broccoli florets

- 1/2 cup carrots, thinly sliced

- 1/4 cup snow peas

- 1/4 cup red bell pepper, thinly sliced

- 1/4 cup yellow bell pepper, thinly sliced

- 1/4 cup green bell pepper, thinly sliced

- 8 ounces rice noodles, cooked according to package instructions

- 1/4 cup tamarind paste

- 1/4 cup water

- 2 tablespoons soy sauce or tamari

- 1 tablespoon rice vinegar

- 1 tablespoon honey or maple syrup

- 1/4 cup chopped peanuts

- 1/4 cup chopped scallions

INSTRUCTIONS

1. Cook the rice noodles. Drain and set aside.

2. Heat a wok or large skillet over high heat. Add the vegetable oil.

3. Add the onion, garlic, and ginger to the wok. Stir-fry for 1-2 minutes, or until fragrant.

4. Add the broccoli, carrots, snow peas, red bell pepper, yellow bell pepper, and green bell pepper to the wok. Stir-fry for 3-4 minutes, or until crisp-tender.

5. Add the cooked rice noodles to the wok. Break them apart with a spatula and stir-fry for 2-3 minutes, or until heated through.

6. Add the tamarind paste, water, soy sauce, rice vinegar, and honey to the wok. Stir-fry for 1 minute, or until the sauce is heated through.

7. Combine the vegetables, noodles, and sauce. Stir-fry for 1 minute more, or until everything is coated in the sauce. Sprinkle with chopped peanuts and scallions and serve immediately.

NOTES

- For a spicier dish, add red pepper flakes.

- To make this dish gluten-free, use tamari instead of soy sauce.

- Serve with a side of stir-fried vegetables or a salad for a complete meal.

NUTRITIONAL INFO (approximate, per serving)

- Calories: 350-400 | Protein: 15-20g | Fat: 15-20g | Carbohydrates: 30-35g | Fiber: 5-7g | Net Carbs: 25-30g

Garlic Wok Noodles

A simple and flavorful vegan dish.

 **Prep Time:** 15 minutes || **Cook Time:** 10 minutes || **Yield:** 4 servings

INGREDIENTS

For the stir-fry:

- 1 tablespoon vegetable oil

- 1 onion, thinly sliced

- 2 cloves garlic, minced

- 1 inch piece ginger, grated

- 1 pound ramen noodles (unseasoned)

- 1/4 cup vegetable broth

- 2 tablespoons soy sauce or tamari

- 1 tablespoon rice vinegar

- 1 teaspoon honey or maple syrup

- 1/4 cup chopped scallions

INSTRUCTIONS

1. Cook the ramen noodles. Drain and set aside.

2. Heat a wok or large skillet over high heat. Add the vegetable oil.

3. Add the onion, garlic, and ginger to the wok. Stir-fry for 1-2 minutes, or until fragrant.

4. Add the cooked ramen noodles to the wok. Break them apart with a spatula and stir-fry for 2-3 minutes, or until heated through.

5. Add the vegetable broth, soy sauce, rice vinegar, and honey to the wok. Stir-fry for 1 minute, or until the sauce is heated through.

6. Combine the noodles with the sauce. Stir-fry for 1 minute more, or until everything is coated in the sauce. Sprinkle with chopped scallions and serve immediately.

NOTES

- To make this dish gluten-free, use tamari instead of soy sauce.

- Serve with a side of stir-fried vegetables or a salad for a complete meal.

NUTRITIONAL INFO (approximate, per serving)

- Calories: 300-350 | Protein: 15-20g | Fat: 10-15g | Carbohydrates: 30-35g | Fiber: 5-7g | Net Carbs: 25-30g

Asparagus and Mushroom Stir-Fry

A quick and flavorful vegan dish.

 **Prep Time:** 15 minutes || **Cook Time:** 10 minutes || **Yield:** 4 servings

INGREDIENTS

For the stir-fry:

- 1 tablespoon vegetable oil

- 1 onion, thinly sliced

- 2 cloves garlic, minced

- 1 inch piece ginger, grated

- 1 bunch asparagus, cut into 2-inch pieces

- 1 pound mixed mushrooms (shiitake, cremini, oyster)

- 1/4 cup vegetable broth

- 2 tablespoons soy sauce or tamari

- 1 tablespoon rice vinegar

- 1 teaspoon honey or maple syrup

INSTRUCTIONS

1. Heat a wok or large skillet over high heat. Add the vegetable oil.

2. Add the onion, garlic, and ginger to the wok. Stir-fry for 1-2 minutes, or until fragrant.

3. Add the asparagus and mushrooms to the wok. Stir-fry for 3-4 minutes, or until crisp-tender.

4. Add the vegetable broth, soy sauce, rice vinegar, and honey to the wok. Stir-fry for 1 minute, or until the sauce is heated through.

5. Combine the vegetables with the sauce. Stir-fry for 1 minute more, or until everything is coated in the sauce. Serve immediately over rice.

NOTES

- For a spicier dish, add red pepper flakes.

- To make this dish gluten-free, use tamari instead of soy sauce.

- Serve over brown rice or cauliflower rice for a complete meal.

NUTRITIONAL INFO (approximate, per serving)

- Calories: 250-300 | Protein: 10-15g | Fat: 15-20g | Carbohydrates: 20-25g | Fiber: 5-7g | Net Carbs: 15-18g

Benihana-Inspired Fried Rice

A flavorful and satisfying vegan dish.

 **Prep Time:** 15 minutes || **Cook Time:** 10 minutes || **Yield:** 4 servings

INGREDIENTS

For the stir-fry:

- 1 tablespoon vegetable oil

- 1 onion, thinly sliced

- 2 cloves garlic, minced

- 1 inch piece ginger, grated

- 1 cup cooked brown rice

- 1/4 cup carrots, thinly sliced

- 1/4 cup peas

- 1/4 cup green onions, chopped

- 1 egg substitute (or scrambled tofu)

- 2 tablespoons soy sauce or tamari

- 1 tablespoon rice vinegar

- 1 teaspoon honey or maple syrup

INSTRUCTIONS

1. Heat a wok or large skillet over high heat. Add the vegetable oil.

2. Add the onion, garlic, and ginger to the wok. Stir-fry for 1-2 minutes, or until fragrant.

3. Add the carrots and peas to the wok. Stir-fry for 2-3 minutes, or until crisp-tender.

4. Add the cooked brown rice to the wok. Break it apart with a spatula and stir-fry for 2-3 minutes, or until heated through.

5. In a separate bowl, scramble the egg substitute or tofu. Add it to the wok and stir-fry until cooked through.

6. Add the soy sauce, rice vinegar, and honey to the wok. Stir-fry for 1 minute, or until the sauce is heated through.

7. Combine all the ingredients in the wok. Stir-fry for 1 minute more, or until everything is coated in the sauce. Sprinkle with green onions and serve immediately.

NOTES

- For a spicier dish, add red pepper flakes to the sauce.

- To make this dish gluten-free, use tamari instead of soy sauce.

- Serve with a side of stir-fried vegetables or a salad for a complete meal.

NUTRITIONAL INFO (approximate, per serving)

- Calories: 350-400 | Protein: 20-25g | Fat: 15-20g | Carbohydrates: 30-35g | Fiber: 5-7g | Net Carbs: 25-30g

Bok Choy and Shiitake Mushroom Stir-Fry

A quick and flavorful vegan dish.

 **Prep Time:** 15 minutes || **Cook Time:** 10 minutes || **Yield:** 4 servings

INGREDIENTS

For the stir-fry:

- 1 tablespoon vegetable oil

- 1 onion, thinly sliced

- 2 cloves garlic, minced

- 1 inch piece ginger, grated

- 1 head bok choy, cut into wedges

- 8 ounces shiitake mushrooms, sliced

- 1/4 cup vegetable broth

- 2 tablespoons soy sauce or tamari

- 1 tablespoon rice vinegar

- 1 teaspoon honey or maple syrup

INSTRUCTIONS

1. Heat a wok or large skillet over high heat. Add the vegetable oil.

2. Add the onion, garlic, and ginger to the wok. Stir-fry for 1-2 minutes, or until fragrant.

3. Add the bok choy and shiitake mushrooms to the wok. Stir-fry for 3-4 minutes, or until crisp-tender.

4. Add the vegetable broth, soy sauce, rice vinegar, and honey to the wok. Stir-fry for 1 minute, or until the sauce is heated through.

5. Combine the vegetables with the sauce. Stir-fry for 1 minute more, or until everything is coated in the sauce. Serve immediately over rice.

NOTES

- For a spicier dish, add red pepper flakes.

- To make this dish gluten-free, use tamari instead of soy sauce.

- Serve over brown rice or cauliflower rice for a complete meal.

NUTRITIONAL INFO (approximate, per serving)

- Calories: 250-300 | Protein: 10-15g | Fat: 10-15g | Carbohydrates: 20-25g | Fiber: 5-7g | Net Carbs: 15-18g

Chinese Eggplant with Garlic Sauce

A classic Chinese dish, made vegan-friendly.

 **Prep Time:** 15 minutes || **Cook Time:** 10 minutes || **Yield:** 4 servings

INGREDIENTS

For the eggplant:

- 1 large eggplant, cubed

- 1 tablespoon cornstarch

- 1/4 teaspoon salt

For the garlic sauce:

- 2 tablespoons soy sauce or tamari

- 1 tablespoon rice vinegar

- 1 tablespoon honey or maple syrup

- 1 tablespoon sesame oil

- 2 cloves garlic, minced

- 1/2 teaspoon red pepper flakes (optional)

For the stir-fry:

- 1 tablespoon vegetable oil

- 1 onion, thinly sliced

- 2 cloves garlic, minced

- 1 inch piece ginger, grated

- 1 red bell pepper, thinly sliced

INSTRUCTIONS

1. Toss the eggplant cubes with cornstarch and salt in a bowl. Set aside.

2. In a small bowl, whisk together the soy sauce, rice vinegar, honey, sesame oil, minced garlic, and red pepper flakes (if using).

3. Heat a wok or large skillet over high heat. Add the vegetable oil.

4. Add the onion, garlic, and ginger to the wok. Stir-fry for 1-2 minutes, or until fragrant.

5. Add the prepared eggplant cubes to the wok. Stir-fry for 3-4 minutes, or until browned and cooked through.

6. Add the red bell pepper to the wok. Stir-fry for 2-3 minutes, or until crisp-tender.

7. Pour the garlic sauce over the vegetables. Stir-fry for 1 minute more, or until everything is coated in the sauce. Serve immediately over rice.

NOTES

- For a spicier dish, add more red pepper flakes.

- To make this dish gluten-free, use tamari instead of soy sauce.

- Serve over brown rice or cauliflower rice for a complete meal.

NUTRITIONAL INFO (approximate, per serving)

- Calories: 250-300 | Protein: 10-15g | Fat: 15-20g | Carbohydrates: 20-25g | Fiber: 5-7g | Net Carbs: 15-18g

Cabbage and Glass Noodle Stir-Fry

A light and flavorful vegan dish.

 **Prep Time:** 15 minutes || **Cook Time:** 10 minutes || **Yield:** 4 servings

INGREDIENTS

For the stir-fry:

- 1 tablespoon vegetable oil

- 1 onion, thinly sliced

- 2 cloves garlic, minced

- 1 inch piece ginger, grated

- 1 head cabbage, shredded

- 8 ounces glass noodles, cooked according to package instructions

- 1/4 cup vegetable broth

- 2 tablespoons soy sauce or tamari

- 1 tablespoon rice vinegar

- 1 teaspoon honey or maple syrup

INSTRUCTIONS

1. Heat a wok or large skillet over high heat. Add the vegetable oil.

2. Add the onion, garlic, and ginger to the wok. Stir-fry for 1-2 minutes, or until fragrant.

3. Add the shredded cabbage to the wok. Stir-fry for 3-4 minutes, or until crisp-tender.

4. Add the cooked glass noodles to the wok. Break them apart with a spatula.

5. Add the vegetable broth, soy sauce, rice vinegar, and honey to the wok. Stir-fry for 1 minute, or until the sauce is heated through.

6. Combine the cabbage, noodles, and sauce. Stir-fry for 1 minute more, or until everything is coated in the sauce. Serve immediately.

NOTES

- For a spicier dish, add red pepper flakes.

- To make this dish gluten-free, use tamari instead of soy sauce.

- Serve over brown rice or cauliflower rice for a complete meal.

NUTRITIONAL INFO (approximate, per serving)

- Calories: 250-300 | Protein: 10-15g | Fat: 10-15g | Carbohydrates: 20-25g | Fiber: 5-7g | Net Carbs: 15-18g

BBQ Tofu Stir-Fry

A smoky and flavorful vegan dish.

 **Prep Time:** 15 minutes ||  **Cook Time:** 10 minutes ||  **Yield:** 4 servings

INGREDIENTS

For the marinade:

- 1 block extra-firm tofu, pressed and cubed

- 1/4 cup barbecue sauce

- 1 tablespoon rice vinegar

- 1/2 teaspoon cornstarch

- 1/4 teaspoon red pepper flakes

- 1/4 teaspoon garlic powder

- 1/4 teaspoon ginger powder

- 1 tablespoon vegetable oil

- 1 onion, thinly sliced

- 2 cloves garlic, minced

- 1 inch piece ginger, grated

- 1 red bell pepper, thinly sliced

- 1/4 cup vegetable broth

- 2 tablespoons soy sauce or tamari

- 1 tablespoon rice vinegar

- 1 teaspoon honey or maple syrup

For the stir-fry:

INSTRUCTIONS

1. In a bowl, combine the tofu cubes with the marinade ingredients. Toss to coat and let marinate for at least 15 minutes, or up to 30 minutes.

2. Heat a wok or large skillet over high heat. Add the vegetable oil.

3. Add the onion, garlic, and ginger to the wok. Stir-fry for 1-2 minutes, or until fragrant.

4. Add the bell pepper to the wok. Stir-fry for 2-3 minutes, or until crisp-tender.

5. Add the marinated tofu to the wok. Stir-fry for 3-4 minutes, or until browned and heated through.

6. Add the vegetable broth, soy sauce, rice vinegar, and honey to the wok. Stir-fry for 1 minute, or until the sauce is heated through.

7. Combine the vegetables and tofu with the sauce. Stir-fry for 1 minute more, or until everything is coated in the sauce. Serve immediately over rice.

NOTES

- For a spicier dish, add more red pepper flakes or use a spicier barbecue sauce.

- To make this dish gluten-free, use tamari instead of soy sauce.

- Serve over brown rice or cauliflower rice for a complete meal.

NUTRITIONAL INFO (approximate, per serving)

- Calories: 300-350 | Protein: 20-25g | Fat: 15-20g | Carbohydrates: 20-25g | Fiber: 5-7g | Net Carbs: 15-18g

Szechuan Tofu Stir-Fry

A spicy and flavorful vegan dish.

 **Prep Time:** 15 minutes || **Cook Time:** 10 minutes || **Yield:** 4 servings

INGREDIENTS

For the marinade:

- 1 block extra-firm tofu, pressed and cubed

- 1 tablespoon soy sauce or tamari

- 1 teaspoon rice vinegar

- 1/2 teaspoon cornstarch

- 1/4 teaspoon red pepper flakes

- 1/4 teaspoon garlic powder

- 1/4 teaspoon ginger powder

For the stir-fry:

- 1 tablespoon vegetable oil

- 1 onion, thinly sliced

- 2 cloves garlic, minced

- 1 inch piece ginger, grated

- 1 red bell pepper, thinly sliced

- 1 tablespoon Sichuan peppercorns

- 1/4 cup vegetable broth

- 2 tablespoons soy sauce or tamari

- 1 tablespoon rice vinegar

- 1 teaspoon honey or maple syrup

INSTRUCTIONS

1. In a bowl, combine the tofu cubes with the marinade ingredients. Toss to coat and let marinate for at least 15 minutes, or up to 30 minutes.

2. Heat a wok or large skillet over high heat. Add the vegetable oil.

3. Add the onion, garlic, and ginger to the wok. Stir-fry for 1-2 minutes, or until fragrant.

4. Add the bell pepper to the wok. Stir-fry for 2-3 minutes, or until crisp-tender.

5. Add the Sichuan peppercorns to the wok. Stir-fry for 1 minute, or until fragrant and slightly toasted.

6. Add the marinated tofu to the wok. Stir-fry for 3-4 minutes, or until browned and heated through.

7. Add the vegetable broth, soy sauce, rice vinegar, and honey to the wok. Stir-fry for 1 minute, or until the sauce is heated through.

8. Combine the vegetables and tofu with the sauce. Stir-fry for 1 minute more, or until everything is coated in the sauce. Serve immediately over rice.

NOTES

- For a spicier dish, add more Sichuan peppercorns or red pepper flakes.

- To make this dish gluten-free, use tamari instead of soy sauce.

- Serve over brown rice or cauliflower rice for a complete meal.

NUTRITIONAL INFO (approximate, per serving)

- Calories: 300-350 | Protein: 20-25g | Fat: 15-20g | Carbohydrates: 20-25g | Fiber: 5-7g | Net Carbs: 15-18g

Black Pepper Tofu Stir-Fry

A spicy and flavorful vegan dish.

 **Prep Time:** 15 minutes || **Cook Time:** 10 minutes || **Yield:** 4 servings

INGREDIENTS

For the marinade:

- 1 block extra-firm tofu, pressed and cubed

- 1 tablespoon soy sauce or tamari

- 1 teaspoon rice vinegar

- 1/2 teaspoon cornstarch

- 1/4 teaspoon red pepper flakes

- 1/4 teaspoon garlic powder

- 1/4 teaspoon ginger powder

For the stir-fry:

- 1 tablespoon vegetable oil

- 1 onion, thinly sliced

- 2 cloves garlic, minced

- 1 inch piece ginger, grated

- 1 red bell pepper, thinly sliced

- 1/4 cup black peppercorns, crushed

- 1/4 cup vegetable broth

- 2 tablespoons soy sauce or tamari

- 1 tablespoon rice vinegar

- 1 teaspoon honey or maple syrup

INSTRUCTIONS

1. In a bowl, combine the tofu cubes with the marinade ingredients. Toss to coat and let marinate for at least 15 minutes, or up to 30 minutes.

2. Heat a wok or large skillet over high heat. Add the vegetable oil.

3. Add the onion, garlic, and ginger to the wok. Stir-fry for 1-2 minutes, or until fragrant.

4. Add the bell pepper to the wok. Stir-fry for 2-3 minutes, or until crisp-tender.

5. Add the marinated tofu to the wok. Stir-fry for 3-4 minutes, or until browned and heated through.

6. Add the crushed black peppercorns to the wok. Stir-fry for 1 minute, or until fragrant.

7. Add the vegetable broth, soy sauce, rice vinegar, and honey to the wok. Stir-fry for 1 minute, or until the sauce is heated through.

8. Combine the vegetables and tofu with the sauce. Stir-fry for 1 minute more, or until everything is coated in the sauce. Serve immediately over rice.

NOTES

- For a spicier dish, add more red pepper flakes or black peppercorns.

- To make this dish gluten-free, use tamari instead of soy sauce.

- Serve over brown rice or cauliflower rice for a complete meal.

NUTRITIONAL INFO (approximate, per serving)

- Calories: 300-350 | Protein: 20-25g | Fat: 15-20g | Carbohydrates: 20-25g | Fiber: 5-7g | Net Carbs: 15-18g

Mushroom Cabbage Stir-Fry

A hearty and flavorful vegan dish.

 **Prep Time:** 15 minutes || **Cook Time:** 10 minutes || **Yield:** 4 servings

INGREDIENTS

For the stir-fry:

- 1 tablespoon vegetable oil

- 1 onion, thinly sliced

- 2 cloves garlic, minced

- 1 inch piece ginger, grated

- 1 head cabbage, shredded

- 1 pound mixed mushrooms (shiitake, cremini, oyster)

- 1/4 cup vegetable broth

- 2 tablespoons soy sauce or tamari

- 1 tablespoon rice vinegar

- 1 teaspoon honey or maple syrup

INSTRUCTIONS

1. Heat a wok or large skillet over high heat. Add the vegetable oil.

2. Add the onion, garlic, and ginger to the wok. Stir-fry for 1-2 minutes, or until fragrant.

3. Add the cabbage and mushrooms to the wok. Stir-fry for 3-4 minutes, or until crisp-tender.

4. Add the vegetable broth, soy sauce, rice vinegar, and honey to the wok. Stir-fry for 1 minute, or until the sauce is heated through.

5. Combine the vegetables with the sauce. Stir-fry for 1 minute more, or until everything is coated in the sauce. Serve immediately over rice.

NOTES

- For a spicier dish, add red pepper flakes.

- To make this dish gluten-free, use tamari instead of soy sauce.

- Serve over brown rice or cauliflower rice for a complete meal.

NUTRITIONAL INFO (approximate, per serving)

- Calories: 250-300 | Protein: 10-15g | Fat: 15-20g | Carbohydrates: 20-25g | Fiber: 5-7g | Net Carbs: 15-18g

Eggplant, Potato, and Pepper Stir-Fry

A hearty and flavorful vegan dish.

 **Prep Time:** 15 minutes || **Cook Time:** 15 minutes || **Yield:** 4 servings

INGREDIENTS

For the stir-fry:

- 1 tablespoon vegetable oil

- 1 onion, thinly sliced

- 2 cloves garlic, minced

- 1 inch piece ginger, grated

- 1 large eggplant, cubed

- 1 medium potato, cubed

- 1 red bell pepper, thinly sliced

- 1/4 cup vegetable broth

- 2 tablespoons soy sauce or tamari

- 1 tablespoon rice vinegar

- 1 teaspoon honey or maple syrup

- 1/4 teaspoon red pepper flakes

INSTRUCTIONS

1. Heat a wok or large skillet over high heat. Add the vegetable oil.

2. Add the onion, garlic, and ginger to the wok. Stir-fry for 1-2 minutes, or until fragrant.

3. Add the eggplant, potato, and bell pepper to the wok. Stir-fry for 5-7 minutes, or until the vegetables are tender-crisp.

4. Add the vegetable broth, soy sauce, rice vinegar, honey, and red pepper flakes to the wok. Stir-fry for 1 minute, or until the sauce is heated through.

5. Combine the vegetables with the sauce. Stir-fry for 1 minute more, or until everything is coated in the sauce. Serve immediately over rice.

NOTES

- To make this dish gluten-free, use tamari instead of soy sauce.

- Serve over brown rice or cauliflower rice for a complete meal.

NUTRITIONAL INFO (approximate, per serving)

- Calories: 300-350 | Protein: 15-20g | Fat: 15-20g | Carbohydrates: 25-30g | Fiber: 5-7g | Net Carbs: 20-25g

Vegetable Yakisoba

Prep Time: 15 minutes || **Cook Time:** 10 minutes || **Yield:** 4 servings

INGREDIENTS

For the stir-fry:

- 1 tablespoon vegetable oil

- 1 onion, thinly sliced

- 2 cloves garlic, minced

- 1 inch piece ginger, grated

- 1 cup broccoli florets

- 1/2 cup carrots, thinly sliced

- 1/4 cup snow peas

- 1/4 cup cabbage, shredded

- 8 ounces yakisoba noodles, cooked

- 1/4 cup teriyaki sauce

- 1 tablespoon soy sauce or tamari

- 1 teaspoon rice vinegar

- 1/2 teaspoon red pepper flakes

- 1/4 cup chopped scallions

INSTRUCTIONS

1. Heat a wok or large skillet over high heat. Add the vegetable oil.

2. Add the onion, garlic, and ginger to the wok. Stir-fry for 1-2 minutes, or until fragrant.

3. Add the broccoli, carrots, snow peas, and cabbage to the wok. Stir-fry for 3-4 minutes.

4. Add the cooked yakisoba noodles to the wok. Break them apart with a spatula.

5. Add the teriyaki sauce, soy sauce, rice vinegar, and red pepper flakes to the wok. Stir-fry for 1 minute, or until the sauce is heated through.

6. Combine the vegetables, noodles, and sauce. Stir-fry for 1 minute more, or until everything is coated in the sauce. Sprinkle with chopped scallions and serve immediately.

NOTES

- To make this dish gluten-free, use gluten-free teriyaki sauce and tamari.

- Serve with a side of stir-fried vegetables or a salad for a complete meal.

NUTRITIONAL INFO (approximate, per serving)

- Calories: 350-400 | Protein: 15-20g | Fat: 15-20g | Carbohydrates: 30-35g | Fiber: 5-7g | Net Carbs: 25-30g

Honey Ginger Tofu Stir-Fry

A sweet and savory vegan dish.

 **Prep Time:** 15 minutes || **Cook Time:** 10 minutes || **Yield:** 4 servings

INGREDIENTS

For the marinade:

- 1 block extra-firm tofu, pressed and cubed

- 1 tablespoon soy sauce or tamari

- 1 teaspoon rice vinegar

- 1/2 teaspoon cornstarch

- 1/4 teaspoon red pepper flakes

- 1/4 teaspoon garlic powder

- 1/4 teaspoon ginger powder

For the stir-fry:

- 1 tablespoon vegetable oil

- 1 onion, thinly sliced

- 2 cloves garlic, minced

- 1 inch piece ginger, grated

- 1 red bell pepper, thinly sliced

- 1/4 cup honey or maple syrup

- 2 tablespoons sesame oil

- 1 tablespoon soy sauce or tamari

- 1 tablespoon rice vinegar

- 1/4 cup chopped sesame seeds

INSTRUCTIONS

1. In a bowl, combine the tofu cubes with the marinade ingredients. Toss to coat and let marinate for at least 15 minutes, or up to 30 minutes.

2. Heat a wok or large skillet over high heat. Add the vegetable oil.

3. Add the onion, garlic, and ginger to the wok. Stir-fry for 1-2 minutes, or until fragrant.

4. Add the bell pepper to the wok. Stir-fry for 2-3 minutes, or until crisp-tender.

5. Add the marinated tofu to the wok. Stir-fry for 3-4 minutes, or until browned and heated through.

6. Add the honey, sesame oil, soy sauce, and rice vinegar to the wok. Stir-fry for 1 minute, or until the sauce is heated through.

7. Combine the vegetables and tofu with the sauce. Stir-fry for 1 minute more, or until everything is coated in the sauce. Sprinkle with sesame seeds and serve immediately over rice.

NOTES

- For a spicier dish, add more red pepper flakes.

- To make this dish gluten-free, use tamari instead of soy sauce.

- Serve over brown rice or cauliflower rice for a complete meal.

NUTRITIONAL INFO (approximate, per serving)

- Calories: 300-350 | Protein: 20-25g | Fat: 15-20g | Carbohydrates: 20-25g | Fiber: 5-7g | Net Carbs: 15-18g

Cauliflower Tofu Fried Rice

A healthy and flavorful vegan option.

 **Prep Time:** 15 minutes || **Cook Time:** 10 minutes || **Yield:** 4 servings

INGREDIENTS

For the stir-fry:

- 1 tablespoon vegetable oil

- 1 onion, thinly sliced

- 2 cloves garlic, minced

- 1 inch piece ginger, grated

- 1 head cauliflower, cut into small florets

- 1 block extra-firm tofu, cubed

- 1 cup cooked brown rice

- 1/4 cup peas

- 1/4 cup carrots, finely chopped

- 1/4 cup vegetable broth

- 2 tablespoons soy sauce or tamari

- 1 tablespoon rice vinegar

- 1 teaspoon honey or maple syrup

- 1/4 cup chopped scallions

INSTRUCTIONS

1. In a small bowl, combine the tofu cubes with 1 tablespoon soy sauce, 1 teaspoon rice vinegar, and 1/2 teaspoon cornstarch. Toss to coat and let marinate for at least 15 minutes, or up to 30 minutes.

2. Heat a wok or large skillet over high heat. Add the vegetable oil.

3. Add the onion, garlic, and ginger to the wok. Stir-fry for 1-2 minutes, or until fragrant.

4. Add the cauliflower florets to the wok. Stir-fry for 3-4 minutes, or until tender-crisp.

5. Add the marinated tofu to the wok. Stir-fry for 3-4 minutes, or until browned and heated through.

6. Add the cooked brown rice, peas, and carrots to the wok. Stir-fry for 2-3 minutes, or until heated through.

7. Add the vegetable broth, soy sauce, rice vinegar, and honey to the wok. Stir-fry for 1 minute, or until the sauce is heated through.

8. Combine all the ingredients in the wok. Stir-fry for 1 minute more, or until everything is coated in the sauce. Sprinkle with chopped scallions and serve immediately.

NOTES

- For a spicier dish, add red pepper flakes to the marinade or sauce.

- To make this dish gluten-free, use tamari instead of soy sauce.

- Serve with a side of stir-fried vegetables or a salad for a complete meal.

NUTRITIONAL INFO (approximate, per serving)

- Calories: 350-400 | Protein: 20-25g | Fat: 15-20g | Carbohydrates: 30-35g | Fiber: 5-7g | Net Carbs: 25-30g

Broccoli and Vegetable Stir-Fry with Garlic Sauce

A quick and easy vegan dish.

 **Prep Time:** 15 minutes || **Cook Time:** 10 minutes || **Yield:** 4 servings

INGREDIENTS

For the stir-fry:

- 1 tablespoon vegetable oil

- 1 onion, thinly sliced

- 2 cloves garlic, minced

- 1 inch piece ginger, grated

- 1 head broccoli, cut into florets

- 1 carrot, thinly sliced

- 1/2 cup snow peas

- 1/4 cup vegetable broth

- 2 tablespoons soy sauce or tamari

- 1 tablespoon rice vinegar

- 1 teaspoon honey or maple syrup

For the garlic sauce:

- 1/4 cup soy sauce or tamari

- 2 tablespoons rice vinegar

- 1 tablespoon honey or maple syrup

- 1 tablespoon sesame oil

- 2 cloves garlic, minced

INSTRUCTIONS

1. In a small bowl, whisk together the soy sauce, rice vinegar, honey, sesame oil, and minced garlic. Set aside.

2. Heat a wok or large skillet over high heat. Add the vegetable oil.

3. Add the onion, garlic, and ginger to the wok. Stir-fry for 1-2 minutes, or until fragrant.

4. Add the broccoli, carrot, and snow peas to the wok. Stir-fry for 3-4 minutes, or until crisp-tender.

5. Pour the prepared garlic sauce over the vegetables. Stir-fry for 1 minute more, or until the sauce coats the vegetables evenly.

6. Serve immediately over rice.

NOTES

- For a spicier dish, add red pepper flakes to the garlic sauce.

- To make this dish gluten-free, use tamari instead of soy sauce.

- Serve over brown rice or cauliflower rice for a complete meal.

NUTRITIONAL INFO (approximate, per serving)

- Calories: 250-300 | Protein: 10-15g | Fat: 10-15g | Carbohydrates: 20-25g | Fiber: 5-7g | Net Carbs: 15-18g

Orange Cauliflower Stir-Fry

A tangy and flavorful vegan dish.

 **Prep Time:** 15 minutes || **Cook Time:** 10 minutes || **Yield:** 4 servings

INGREDIENTS

For the stir-fry:

- 1 tablespoon vegetable oil

- 1 onion, thinly sliced

- 2 cloves garlic, minced

- 1 inch piece ginger, grated

- 1 head cauliflower, cut into florets

- 1/2 cup orange juice

- 1/4 cup orange zest

- 2 tablespoons soy sauce or tamari

- 1 tablespoon rice vinegar

- 1 teaspoon honey or maple syrup

- 1/2 teaspoon red pepper flakes

INSTRUCTIONS

1. Heat a wok or large skillet over high heat. Add the vegetable oil.

2. Add the onion, garlic, and ginger to the wok. Stir-fry for 1-2 minutes, or until fragrant.

3. Add the cauliflower florets to the wok. Stir-fry for 3-4 minutes, or until crisp-tender.

4. Add the orange juice, orange zest, soy sauce, rice vinegar, honey, and red pepper flakes to the wok. Stir-fry for 1 minute, or until the sauce is heated through.

5. Combine the cauliflower with the sauce. Stir-fry for 1 minute more, or until everything is coated in the sauce. Serve immediately over rice.

NOTES

- For a spicier dish, add more red pepper flakes.

- To make this dish gluten-free, use tamari instead of soy sauce.

- Serve over brown rice or cauliflower rice for a complete meal.

NUTRITIONAL INFO (approximate, per serving)

- Calories: 250-300 | Protein: 10-15g | Fat: 10-15g | Carbohydrates: 20-25g | Fiber: 5-7g | Net Carbs: 15-18g

Teriyaki Mixed Vegetable Stir-Fry

A quick and easy vegan dish.

 **Prep Time:** 15 minutes || **Cook Time:** 10 minutes || **Yield:** 4 servings

INGREDIENTS

For the stir-fry:

- 1 tablespoon vegetable oil

- 1 onion, thinly sliced

- 2 cloves garlic, minced

- 1 inch piece ginger, grated

- 1 cup broccoli florets

- 1/2 cup snow peas

- 1/2 cup carrots, thinly sliced

- 1/4 cup bell pepper, thinly sliced

- 1/4 cup teriyaki sauce

- 1 tablespoon rice vinegar

- 1 teaspoon honey or maple syrup

- 1/4 cup chopped scallions

INSTRUCTIONS

1. Heat a wok or large skillet over high heat. Add the vegetable oil.

2. Add the onion, garlic, and ginger to the wok. Stir-fry for 1-2 minutes, or until fragrant.

3. Add the broccoli, snow peas, carrots, and bell pepper to the wok. Stir-fry for 3-4 minutes, or until crisp-tender.

4. Add the teriyaki sauce, rice vinegar, and honey to the wok. Stir-fry for 1 minute, or until the sauce is heated through.

5. Combine the vegetables with the sauce. Stir-fry for 1 minute more, or until everything is coated in the sauce. Sprinkle with chopped scallions and serve immediately over rice.

NOTES

- To make this dish gluten-free, use a gluten-free teriyaki sauce.

- Serve over brown rice or cauliflower rice for a complete meal.

NUTRITIONAL INFO (approximate, per serving)

- Calories: 250-300 | Protein: 10-15g | Fat: 15-20g | Carbohydrates: 20-25g | Fiber: 5-7g | Net Carbs: 15-18g

Teriyaki Cauliflower Stir-Fry

A quick and easy vegan dish.

**Prep Time:** 15 minutes || **Cook Time:** 10 minutes || **Yield:** 4 servings

INGREDIENTS

For the stir-fry:

- 1 tablespoon vegetable oil

- 1 onion, thinly sliced

- 2 cloves garlic, minced

- 1 inch piece ginger, grated

- 1 head cauliflower, cut into florets

- 1/4 cup teriyaki sauce

- 1 tablespoon rice vinegar

- 1 teaspoon honey or maple syrup

- 1/4 cup chopped scallions

INSTRUCTIONS

1. Heat a wok or large skillet over high heat. Add the vegetable oil.

2. Add the onion, garlic, and ginger to the wok. Stir-fry for 1-2 minutes, or until fragrant.

3. Add the cauliflower florets to the wok. Stir-fry for 3-4 minutes, or until tender-crisp.

4. Add the teriyaki sauce, rice vinegar, and honey to the wok. Stir-fry for 1 minute, or until the sauce is heated through.

5. Combine the cauliflower with the sauce. Stir-fry for 1 minute more, or until everything is coated in the sauce. Sprinkle with chopped scallions and serve immediately over rice.

NOTES

- For a spicier dish, add red pepper flakes to the teriyaki sauce.

- To make this dish gluten-free, use a gluten-free teriyaki sauce.

- Serve over brown rice or cauliflower rice for a complete meal.

NUTRITIONAL INFO (approximate, per serving)

- Calories: 250-300 | Protein: 10-15g | Fat: 15-20g | Carbohydrates: 20-25g | Fiber: 5-7g | Net Carbs: 15-18g

Teriyaki Mushroom Stir-Fry

A quick and easy vegan dish.

 **Prep Time:** 15 minutes || **Cook Time:** 10 minutes || **Yield:** 4 servings

INGREDIENTS

For the stir-fry:

- 1 tablespoon vegetable oil

- 1 onion, thinly sliced

- 2 cloves garlic, minced

- 1 inch piece ginger, grated

- 1 pound mixed mushrooms (shiitake, cremini, oyster)

- 1/4 cup teriyaki sauce

- 1 tablespoon rice vinegar

- 1 teaspoon honey or maple syrup

- 1/4 cup chopped scallions

INSTRUCTIONS

1. Heat a wok or large skillet over high heat. Add the vegetable oil.

2. Add the onion, garlic, and ginger to the wok. Stir-fry for 1-2 minutes, or until fragrant.

3. Add the mixed mushrooms to the wok. Stir-fry for 3-4 minutes, or until cooked through and slightly browned.

4. Add the teriyaki sauce, rice vinegar, and honey to the wok. Stir-fry for 1 minute, or until the sauce is heated through.

5. Combine the mushrooms with the sauce. Stir-fry for 1 minute more, or until everything is coated in the sauce. Sprinkle with chopped scallions and serve immediately over rice.

NOTES

- For a spicier dish, add red pepper flakes to the teriyaki sauce.

- To make this dish gluten-free, use a gluten-free teriyaki sauce.

- Serve over brown rice or cauliflower rice for a complete meal.

NUTRITIONAL INFO (approximate, per serving)

- Calories: 250-300 | Protein: 10-15g | Fat: 15-20g | Carbohydrates: 20-25g | Fiber: 5-7g | Net Carbs: 15-18g

Broccoli Tofu Stir-Fry

A simple and flavorful vegan dish.

 **Prep Time:** 15 minutes || **Cook Time:** 10 minutes || **Yield:** 4 servings

INGREDIENTS

For the marinade:

- 1 block extra-firm tofu, pressed and cubed

- 1 tablespoon soy sauce or tamari

- 1 teaspoon rice vinegar

- 1/2 teaspoon cornstarch

- 1/4 teaspoon red pepper flakes

- 1/4 teaspoon garlic powder

- 1/4 teaspoon ginger powder

- 1 tablespoon vegetable oil

- 1 onion, thinly sliced

- 2 cloves garlic, minced

- 1 inch piece ginger, grated

- 1 head broccoli, cut into florets

- 1/4 cup vegetable broth

- 2 tablespoons soy sauce or tamari

- 1 tablespoon rice vinegar

- 1 teaspoon honey or maple syrup

For the stir-fry:

INSTRUCTIONS

1. In a bowl, combine the tofu cubes with the marinade ingredients. Toss to coat and let marinate for at least 15 minutes, or up to 30 minutes.

2. Heat a wok or large skillet over high heat. Add the vegetable oil.

3. Add the onion, garlic, and ginger to the wok. Stir-fry for 1-2 minutes, or until fragrant.

4. Add the broccoli florets to the wok. Stir-fry for 3-4 minutes, or until crisp-tender.

5. Add the marinated tofu to the wok. Stir-fry for 3-4 minutes, or until browned and heated through.

6. Add the vegetable broth, soy sauce, rice vinegar, and honey to the wok. Stir-fry for 1 minute, or until the sauce is heated through.

7. Combine the broccoli and tofu with the sauce. Stir-fry for 1 minute more, or until everything is coated in the sauce. Serve immediately over rice.

NOTES

- For a spicier dish, add more red pepper flakes.

- To make this dish gluten-free, use tamari instead of soy sauce.

- Serve over brown rice or cauliflower rice for a complete meal.

NUTRITIONAL INFO (approximate, per serving)

- Calories: 250-300 | Protein: 20-25g | Fat: 10-15g | Carbohydrates: 20-25g | Fiber: 5-7g | Net Carbs: 15-18g

Cabbage and Veggie Stir-Fry

A simple and flavorful vegan dish.

Prep Time: 15 minutes || **Cook Time:** 10 minutes || **Yield:** 4 servings

INGREDIENTS

For the stir-fry:

- 1 tablespoon vegetable oil

- 1 onion, thinly sliced

- 2 cloves garlic, minced

- 1 inch piece ginger, grated

- 1/2 head green cabbage, shredded

- 1 carrot, thinly sliced

- 1 cup broccoli florets

- 1/4 cup snow peas

- 1/4 cup vegetable broth

- 2 tablespoons soy sauce or tamari

- 1 tablespoon rice vinegar

- 1 teaspoon honey or maple syrup

INSTRUCTIONS

1. Heat a wok or large skillet over high heat. Add the vegetable oil.

2. Add the onion, garlic, and ginger to the wok. Stir-fry for 1-2 minutes, or until fragrant.

3. Add the cabbage, carrot, broccoli, and snow peas to the wok. Stir-fry for 3-4 minutes, or until crisp-tender.

4. Add the vegetable broth, soy sauce, rice vinegar, and honey to the wok Stir-fry for 1 minute, or until the sauce is heated through.

5. Combine the vegetables with the sauce. Stir-fry for 1 minute more, or until everything is coated in the sauce. Serve immediately over rice.

NOTES

- To make this dish gluten-free, use tamari instead of soy sauce.

- Serve over brown rice or cauliflower rice for a complete meal.

NUTRITIONAL INFO (approximate, per serving)

- Calories: 250-300 | Protein: 10-15g | Fat: 10-15g | Carbohydrates: 20-25g | Fiber: 5-7g | Net Carbs: 15-18g

Cashew Veggie Stir-Fry

A creamy and flavorful vegan dish.

 **Prep Time:** 15 minutes || **Cook Time:** 10 minutes || **Yield:** 4 servings

INGREDIENTS

For the stir-fry:

- 1 tablespoon vegetable oil

- 1 onion, thinly sliced

- 2 cloves garlic, minced

- 1 inch piece ginger, grated

- 1 red bell pepper, thinly sliced

- 1 cup broccoli florets

- 1/4 cup snow peas

- 1/4 cup cashews

- 1/4 cup vegetable broth

- 2 tablespoons soy sauce or tamari

- 1 tablespoon rice vinegar

- 1 tablespoon honey or maple syrup

- 1/4 cup creamy cashew butter

INSTRUCTIONS

1. Heat a wok or large skillet over high heat. Add the vegetable oil.

2. Add the onion, garlic, and ginger to the wok. Stir-fry for 1-2 minutes, or until fragrant.

3. Add the bell pepper, broccoli, and snow peas to the wok. Stir-fry for 2-3 minutes, or until crisp-tender. Add the cashews to the wok. Stir-fry for 1 minute, or until toasted.

4. Add the vegetable broth, soy sauce, rice vinegar, honey, and cashew butter to the wok. Stir-fry for 1 minute, or until the sauce is heated through and creamy.

5. Combine the vegetables and cashews with the sauce. Stir-fry for 1 minute more, or until everything is coated in the sauce. Serve immediately over rice.

NOTES

- To make this dish gluten-free, use tamari instead of soy sauce.

- Serve over brown rice or cauliflower rice for a complete meal.

NUTRITIONAL INFO (approximate, per serving)

- Calories: 350-400 | Protein: 15-20g | Fat: 20-25g | Carbohydrates: 20-25g | Fiber: 5-7g | Net Carbs: 15-18g

Tamarind Tempeh Stir-Fry

A tangy and flavorful vegan dish.

 **Prep Time:** 15 minutes || **Cook Time:** 10 minutes || **Yield:** 4 servings

INGREDIENTS

For the marinade:

- 1 block tempeh, pressed and crumbled

- 1 tablespoon soy sauce or tamari

- 1 teaspoon rice vinegar

- 1/2 teaspoon cornstarch

- 1/4 teaspoon red pepper flakes

- 1/4 teaspoon garlic powder

- 1/4 teaspoon ginger powder

For the stir-fry:

- 1 tablespoon vegetable oil

- 1 onion, thinly sliced

- 2 cloves garlic, minced

- 1 inch piece ginger, grated

- 1 red bell pepper, thinly sliced

- 1/4 cup tamarind paste

- 1/4 cup water

- 2 tablespoons soy sauce or tamari

- 1 tablespoon rice vinegar

- 1 tablespoon honey or maple syrup

INSTRUCTIONS

1. In a bowl, combine the tempeh with the marinade ingredients. Toss to coat and let marinate for at least 15 minutes, or up to 30 minutes.

2. Heat a wok or large skillet over high heat. Add the vegetable oil.

3. Add the onion, garlic, and ginger to the wok. Stir-fry for 1-2 minutes, or until fragrant.

4. Add the bell pepper to the wok. Stir-fry for 2-3 minutes, or until crisp-tender.

5. Add the marinated tempeh to the wok. Stir-fry for 3-4 minutes, or until browned and heated through.

6. Add the tamarind paste, water, soy sauce, rice vinegar, and honey to the wok. Stir-fry for 1 minute, or until the sauce is heated through.

7. Combine the vegetables and tempeh with the sauce. Stir-fry for 1 minute more, or until everything is coated in the sauce. Serve immediately over rice.

NOTES

- For a spicier dish, add more red pepper flakes.

- To make this dish gluten-free, use tamari instead of soy sauce.

- Serve over brown rice or cauliflower rice for a complete meal.

NUTRITIONAL INFO (approximate, per serving)

- Calories: 300-350 | Protein: 20-25g | Fat: 15-20g | Carbohydrates: 20-25g | Fiber: 5-7g | Net Carbs: 15-18g

Honey Sesame Tofu Stir-Fry

A sweet and savory vegan dish.

 **Prep Time:** 15 minutes || **Cook Time:** 10 minutes || **Yield:** 4 servings

INGREDIENTS

For the marinade:

- 1 block extra-firm tofu, pressed and cubed

- 1 tablespoon soy sauce or tamari

- 1 teaspoon rice vinegar

- 1/2 teaspoon cornstarch

- 1/4 teaspoon red pepper flakes

- 1/4 teaspoon garlic powder

- 1/4 teaspoon ginger powder

For the stir-fry:

- 1 tablespoon vegetable oil

- 1 onion, thinly sliced

- 2 cloves garlic, minced

- 1 inch piece ginger, grated

- 1 red bell pepper, thinly sliced

- 1/4 cup honey or maple syrup

- 2 tablespoons sesame oil

- 1 tablespoon soy sauce or tamari

- 1 tablespoon rice vinegar

- 1/4 cup chopped sesame seeds

INSTRUCTIONS

1. In a bowl, combine the tofu cubes with the marinade ingredients. Toss to coat and let marinate for at least 15 minutes, or up to 30 minutes.

2. Heat a wok or large skillet over high heat. Add the vegetable oil.

3. Add the onion, garlic, and ginger to the wok. Stir-fry for 1-2 minutes, or until fragrant.

4. Add the bell pepper to the wok. Stir-fry for 2-3 minutes, or until crisp-tender.

5. Add the marinated tofu to the wok. Stir-fry for 3-4 minutes, or until browned and heated through.

6. Add the honey, sesame oil, soy sauce, and rice vinegar to the wok. Stir-fry for 1 minute, or until the sauce is heated through.

7. Combine the vegetables and tofu with the sauce. Stir-fry for 1 minute more, or until everything is coated in the sauce. Sprinkle with sesame seeds and serve immediately over rice.

NOTES

- For a spicier dish, add more red pepper flakes.

- To make this dish gluten-free, use tamari instead of soy sauce.

- Serve over brown rice or cauliflower rice for a complete meal.

NUTRITIONAL INFO (approximate, per serving)

- Calories: 300-350 | Protein: 20-25g | Fat: 15-20g | Carbohydrates: 20-25g | Fiber: 5-7g | Net Carbs: 15-18g

Pineapple and "Pork" Stir-Fry

A sweet and savory vegan dish.

 **Prep Time:** 15 minutes || **Cook Time:** 10 minutes || **Yield:** 4 servings

INGREDIENTS

For the "pork":

- 1 block extra-firm tofu, pressed and crumbled

- 1 tablespoon soy sauce or tamari

- 1 teaspoon rice vinegar

- 1/2 teaspoon cornstarch

- 1/4 teaspoon red pepper flakes

- 1/4 teaspoon garlic powder

- 1/4 teaspoon ginger powder

- 1 tablespoon pineapple juice

- 1 tablespoon vegetable oil

- 1 onion, thinly sliced

- 2 cloves garlic, minced

- 1 inch piece ginger, grated

- 1 can (14.5 oz) pineapple chunks, drained

- 1/4 cup vegetable broth

- 2 tablespoons soy sauce or tamari

- 1 tablespoon rice vinegar

- 1 tablespoon honey or maple syrup

- 1/2 teaspoon red pepper flakes

For the stir-fry:

INSTRUCTIONS

1. In a bowl, combine the crumbled tofu with the marinade ingredients. Toss to coat and let marinate for at least 15 minutes, or up to 30 minutes.

2. Heat a wok or large skillet over high heat. Add the vegetable oil.

3. Add the onion, garlic, and ginger to the wok. Stir-fry for 1-2 minutes, or until fragrant.

4. Add the marinated tofu to the wok. Stir-fry for 3-4 minutes, or until browned and heated through.

5. Add the pineapple chunks to the wok. Stir-fry for 1-2 minutes, or until heated through.

6. Add the vegetable broth, soy sauce, rice vinegar, honey, and red pepper flakes to the wok. Stir-fry for 1 minute, or until the sauce is heated through.

7. Combine the "pork," pineapple, and sauce. Stir-fry for 1 minute more, or until everything is coated in the sauce. Serve immediately over rice.

NOTES

- For a spicier dish, add more red pepper flakes.

- To make this dish gluten-free, use tamari instead of soy sauce.

- Serve over brown rice or cauliflower rice for a complete meal.

NUTRITIONAL INFO (approximate, per serving)

- Calories: 300-350 | Protein: 20-25g | Fat: 15-20g | Carbohydrates: 20-25g | Fiber: 5-7g | Net Carbs: 15-18g

Lemongrass Tofu Stir-Fry

A refreshing and flavorful vegan dish.

 **Prep Time:** 15 minutes || **Cook Time:** 10 minutes || **Yield:** 4 servings

INGREDIENTS

For the marinade:

- 1 block extra-firm tofu, pressed and cubed

- 1 tablespoon soy sauce or tamari

- 1 teaspoon rice vinegar

- 1/2 teaspoon cornstarch

- 1/4 teaspoon red pepper flakes

- 1/4 teaspoon garlic powder

- 1/4 teaspoon ginger powder

- 1 onion, thinly sliced

- 2 cloves garlic, minced

- 1 inch piece ginger, grated

- 1 stalk lemongrass, finely chopped

- 1 red bell pepper, thinly sliced

- 1/4 cup vegetable broth

- 2 tablespoons soy sauce or tamari

- 1 tablespoon rice vinegar

- 1 teaspoon honey or maple syrup

- 1/2 teaspoon red pepper flakes

For the stir-fry:

- 1 tablespoon vegetable oil

INSTRUCTIONS

1. In a bowl, combine the tofu cubes with the marinade ingredients. Toss to coat and let marinate for at least 15 minutes, or up to 30 minutes.

2. Heat a wok or large skillet over high heat. Add the vegetable oil.

3. Add the onion, garlic, ginger, and lemongrass to the wok. Stir-fry for 1-2 minutes, or until fragrant.

4. Add the bell pepper to the wok. Stir-fry for 2-3 minutes, or until crisp-tender.

5. Add the marinated tofu to the wok. Stir-fry for 3-4 minutes, or until browned and heated through.

6. Add the vegetable broth, soy sauce, rice vinegar, honey, and red pepper flakes to the wok. Stir-fry for 1 minute, or until the sauce is heated through.

7. Combine the vegetables and tofu with the sauce. Stir-fry for 1 minute more, or until everything is coated in the sauce. Serve immediately over rice.

NOTES

- For a spicier dish, add more red pepper flakes.

- To make this dish gluten-free, use tamari instead of soy sauce.

- Serve over brown rice or cauliflower rice for a complete meal.

NUTRITIONAL INFO (approximate, per serving)

- Calories: 300-350 | Protein: 20-25g | Fat: 15-20g | Carbohydrates: 20-25g | Fiber: 5-7g | Net Carbs: 15-18g

Teriyaki Tofu Stir-Fry

A classic Japanese dish, made vegan-friendly with tofu.

 **Prep Time:** 15 minutes || **Cook Time:** 10 minutes || **Yield:** 4 servings

INGREDIENTS

For the marinade:

- 1 block extra-firm tofu, pressed and cubed

- 1/4 cup teriyaki sauce

- 1 tablespoon rice vinegar

- 1/2 teaspoon cornstarch

- 1/4 teaspoon red pepper flakes

- 1/4 teaspoon garlic powder

- 1/4 teaspoon ginger powder

- 1 tablespoon vegetable oil

- 1 onion, thinly sliced

- 2 cloves garlic, minced

- 1 inch piece ginger, grated

- 1 red bell pepper, thinly sliced

- 1/4 cup broccoli florets

- 1/4 cup snow peas

- 1/4 cup teriyaki sauce

- 1 tablespoon water

For the stir-fry:

INSTRUCTIONS

1. In a bowl, combine the tofu cubes with the marinade ingredients. Toss to coat and let marinate for at least 15 minutes, or up to 30 minutes.

2. Heat a wok or large skillet over high heat. Add the vegetable oil.

3. Add the onion, garlic, and ginger to the wok. Stir-fry for 1-2 minutes, or until fragrant.

4. Add the bell pepper, broccoli, and snow peas to the wok. Stir-fry for 2-3 minutes, or until crisp-tender.

5. Add the marinated tofu to the wok. Stir-fry for 3-4 minutes, or until browned and heated through.

6. Add the teriyaki sauce and water to the wok. Stir-fry for 1 minute, or until the sauce is heated through.

7. Combine the vegetables and tofu with the sauce. Stir-fry for 1 minute more, or until everything is coated in the sauce. Serve immediately over rice.

NOTES

- For a spicier dish, add more red pepper flakes.

- To make this dish gluten-free, use a gluten-free teriyaki sauce.

- Serve over brown rice or cauliflower rice for a complete meal.

NUTRITIONAL INFO (approximate, per serving)

- Calories: 300-350 | Protein: 20-25g | Fat: 15-20g | Carbohydrates: 20-25g | Fiber: 5-7g | Net Carbs: 15-18g

Spicy Orange Tofu Stir-Fry

A tangy and flavorful vegan dish.

 **Prep Time:** 15 minutes || **Cook Time:** 10 minutes || **Yield:** 4 servings

INGREDIENTS

For the marinade:

- 1 block extra-firm tofu, pressed and cubed

- 1 tablespoon soy sauce or tamari

- 1 teaspoon rice vinegar

- 1/2 teaspoon cornstarch

- 1/4 teaspoon red pepper flakes

- 1/4 teaspoon garlic powder

- 1/4 teaspoon ginger powder

For the stir-fry:

- 1 tablespoon vegetable oil

- 1 onion, thinly sliced

- 2 cloves garlic, minced

- 1 inch piece ginger, grated

- 1 red bell pepper, thinly sliced

- 1/2 cup orange juice

- 1/4 cup orange zest

- 2 tablespoons soy sauce or tamari

- 1 tablespoon rice vinegar

- 1 tablespoon honey or maple syrup

- 1/2 teaspoon red pepper flakes

INSTRUCTIONS

1. In a bowl, combine the tofu cubes with the marinade ingredients. Toss to coat and let marinate for at least 15 minutes, or up to 30 minutes.

2. Heat a wok or large skillet over high heat. Add the vegetable oil.

3. Add the onion, garlic, and ginger to the wok. Stir-fry for 1-2 minutes, or until fragrant.

4. Add the bell pepper to the wok. Stir-fry for 2-3 minutes, or until crisp-tender.

5. Add the marinated tofu to the wok. Stir-fry for 3-4 minutes, or until browned and heated through.

6. Add the orange juice, orange zest, soy sauce, rice vinegar, honey, and red pepper flakes to the wok. Stir-fry for 1 minute, or until the sauce is heated through.

7. Combine the vegetables and tofu with the sauce. Stir-fry for 1 minute more, or until everything is coated in the sauce. Serve immediately over rice.

NOTES

- For a spicier dish, add more red pepper flakes.

- To make this dish gluten-free, use tamari instead of soy sauce.

- Serve over brown rice or cauliflower rice for a complete meal.

NUTRITIONAL INFO (approximate, per serving)

- Calories: 300-350 | Protein: 20-25g | Fat: 15-20g | Carbohydrates: 20-25g | Fiber: 5-7g | Net Carbs: 15-18g

Tofu and Green Bean Stir-Fry

A quick and easy vegan dish.

 **Prep Time:** 15 minutes || **Cook Time:** 10 minutes || **Yield:** 4 servings

INGREDIENTS

For the marinade:

- 1 block extra-firm tofu, pressed and cubed

- 1 tablespoon soy sauce or tamari

- 1 teaspoon rice vinegar

- 1/2 teaspoon cornstarch

- 1/4 teaspoon red pepper flakes

- 1/4 teaspoon garlic powder

- 1/4 teaspoon ginger powder

- 1 tablespoon vegetable oil

- 1 onion, thinly sliced

- 2 cloves garlic, minced

- 1 inch piece ginger, grated

- 1 pound green beans, trimmed

- 1/4 cup vegetable broth

- 2 tablespoons soy sauce or tamari

- 1 tablespoon rice vinegar

- 1 teaspoon honey or maple syrup

For the stir-fry:

INSTRUCTIONS

1. In a bowl, combine the tofu cubes with the marinade ingredients. Toss to coat and let marinate for at least 15 minutes, or up to 30 minutes.

2. Heat a wok or large skillet over high heat. Add the vegetable oil.

3. Add the onion, garlic, and ginger to the wok. Stir-fry for 1-2 minutes, or until fragrant.

4. Add the green beans to the wok. Stir-fry for 3-4 minutes, or until crisp-tender.

5. Add the marinated tofu to the wok. Stir-fry for 3-4 minutes, or until browned and heated through.

6. Add the vegetable broth, soy sauce, rice vinegar, and honey to the wok. Stir-fry for 1 minute, or until the sauce is heated through.

7. Combine the green beans and tofu with the sauce. Stir-fry for 1 minute more, or until everything is coated in the sauce. Serve immediately over rice.

NOTES

- For a spicier dish, add more red pepper flakes.

- To make this dish gluten-free, use tamari instead of soy sauce.

- Serve over brown rice or cauliflower rice for a complete meal.

NUTRITIONAL INFO (approximate, per serving)

- Calories: 250-300 | Protein: 20-25g | Fat: 10-15g | Carbohydrates: 20-25g | Fiber: 5-7g | Net Carbs: 15-18g

Ginger-Garlic Vegetable Stir-Fry

A quick and flavorful vegan dish.

 **Prep Time:** 15 minutes || **Cook Time:** 10 minutes || **Yield:** 4 servings

INGREDIENTS

For the stir-fry:

- 1 tablespoon vegetable oil

- 1 onion, thinly sliced

- 2 cloves garlic, minced

- 1 inch piece ginger, grated

- 1 red bell pepper, thinly sliced

- 1 carrot, thinly sliced

- 1 cup broccoli florets

- 1/4 cup snow peas

- 1/4 cup vegetable broth

- 2 tablespoons soy sauce or tamari

- 1 tablespoon rice vinegar

- 1 teaspoon honey or maple syrup

INSTRUCTIONS

1. Heat a wok or large skillet over high heat. Add the vegetable oil.

2. Add the onion, garlic, and ginger to the wok. Stir-fry for 1-2 minutes, or until fragrant.

3. Add the bell pepper, carrot, broccoli, and snow peas to the wok. Stir-fry for 2-3 minutes, or until crisp-tender.

4. Add the vegetable broth, soy sauce, rice vinegar, and honey to the wok. Stir-fry for 1 minute, or until the sauce is heated through.

5. Combine the vegetables with the sauce. Stir-fry for 1 minute more, or until everything is coated in the sauce. Serve immediately over rice.

NOTES

- To make this dish gluten-free, use tamari instead of soy sauce.

- Serve over brown rice or cauliflower rice for a complete meal.

NUTRITIONAL INFO (approximate, per serving)

- Calories: 250-300 | Protein: 10-15g | Fat: 10-15g | Carbohydrates: 20-25g | Fiber: 5-7g | Net Carbs: 15-18g

Cashew Tofu Stir-Fry

A creamy and flavorful vegan stir-fry.

 **Prep Time:** 15 minutes || **Cook Time:** 10 minutes || **Yield:** 4 servings

INGREDIENTS

For the marinade:

- 1 block extra-firm tofu, pressed and cubed

- 1 tablespoon soy sauce or tamari

- 1 teaspoon rice vinegar

- 1/2 teaspoon cornstarch

- 1/4 teaspoon red pepper flakes

- 1/4 teaspoon garlic powder

- 1/4 teaspoon ginger powder

For the stir-fry:

- 1 tablespoon vegetable oil

- 1/2 onion, thinly sliced

- 2 cloves garlic, minced

- 1 inch piece ginger, grated

- 1 red bell pepper, thinly sliced

- 1/2 cup cashews

- 1/4 cup vegetable broth

- 2 tablespoons soy sauce or tamari

- 1 tablespoon rice vinegar

- 1 tablespoon honey or maple syrup

- 1/4 cup creamy cashew butter

INSTRUCTIONS

1. In a bowl, combine the tofu cubes with the marinade ingredients. Toss to coat and let marinate for at least 15 minutes, or up to 30 minutes.

2. Heat a wok or large skillet over high heat. Add the vegetable oil.

3. Add the onion, garlic, and ginger to the wok. Stir-fry for 1-2 minutes, or until fragrant.

4. Add the bell pepper to the wok. Stir-fry for 2-3 minutes, or until crisp-tender.

5. Add the marinated tofu to the wok. Stir-fry for 3-4 minutes, or until browned and heated through.

6. Add the cashews to the wok. Stir-fry for 1 minute, or until toasted.

7. Add the vegetable broth, soy sauce, rice vinegar, honey, and cashew butter to the wok. Stir-fry for 1 minute, or until the sauce is heated through and creamy.

8. Combine the vegetables, tofu, and cashews with the sauce. Stir-fry for 1 minute more, or until everything is coated in the sauce. Serve immediately over rice.

NOTES

- For a spicier dish, add more red pepper flakes.

- To make this dish gluten-free, use tamari instead of soy sauce.

- Serve over brown rice or cauliflower rice for a complete meal.

NUTRITIONAL INFO (approximate, per serving)

- Calories: 350-400 | Protein: 20-25g | Fat: 20-25g | Carbohydrates: 20-25g | Fiber: 5-7g | Net Carbs: 15-18g

Thai Basil Tofu Stir-Fry

A flavorful and aromatic Thai dish.

 **Prep Time:** 15 minutes || **Cook Time:** 10 minutes || **Yield:** 4 servings

INGREDIENTS

For the marinade:

- 1 block extra-firm tofu, pressed and cubed

- 1 tablespoon soy sauce or tamari

- 1 teaspoon rice vinegar

- 1/2 teaspoon cornstarch

- 1/4 teaspoon red pepper flakes

- 1/4 teaspoon garlic powder

- 1/4 teaspoon ginger powder

For the stir-fry:

- 1 tablespoon vegetable oil

- 1/2 onion, thinly sliced

- 2 cloves garlic, minced

- 1 inch piece ginger, grated

- 1 red bell pepper, thinly sliced

- 1 cup Thai basil leaves

- 1/4 cup vegetable broth

- 2 tablespoons soy sauce or tamari

- 1 tablespoon rice vinegar

- 1 teaspoon brown sugar or agave nectar

- 1/2 teaspoon red pepper flakes

INSTRUCTIONS

1. In a bowl, combine the tofu cubes with the marinade ingredients. Toss to coat and let marinate for at least 15 minutes, or up to 30 minutes.

2. Heat a wok or large skillet over high heat. Add the vegetable oil.

3. Add the onion, garlic, and ginger to the wok. Stir-fry for 1-2 minutes, or until fragrant.

4. Add the bell pepper to the wok. Stir-fry for 2-3 minutes, or until crisp-tender.

5. Add the marinated tofu to the wok. Stir-fry for 3-4 minutes, or until browned and heated through.

6. Add the vegetable broth, soy sauce, rice vinegar, brown sugar, and red pepper flakes to the wok. Stir-fry for 1 minute, or until the sauce is heated through.

7. Add the Thai basil leaves to the wok. Stir-fry for 30 seconds, or until the basil is wilted but still retains its bright green color.

8. Serve immediately over rice.

NOTES

- For a spicier dish, add more red pepper flakes.

- To make this dish gluten-free, use tamari instead of soy sauce.

- Serve over brown rice or cauliflower rice for a complete meal.

NUTRITIONAL INFO (approximate, per serving)

- Calories: 300-350 | Protein: 20-25g | Fat: 15-20g | Carbohydrates: 20-25g | Fiber: 5-7g | Net Carbs: 15-18g

Tempeh and Broccoli Stir-Fry

A hearty and nutritious plant-based dish.

 **Prep Time:** 15 minutes || **Cook Time:** 10 minutes || **Yield:** 4 servings

INGREDIENTS

For the marinade:

- 1 block tempeh, pressed and crumbled

- 1 tablespoon soy sauce or tamari

- 1 teaspoon rice vinegar

- 1/2 teaspoon cornstarch

- 1/4 teaspoon red pepper flakes

- 1/4 teaspoon garlic powder

- 1/4 teaspoon ginger powder

- 1 tablespoon sesame oil

- 1 large head of broccoli, cut into florets

- 1 red bell pepper, sliced

- 1 carrot, sliced

- 1/4 cup snow peas

- 2 cloves garlic, minced

- 1 tablespoon soy sauce or tamari

- 1 teaspoon rice vinegar

- 1/2 teaspoon honey or maple syrup

For the stir-fry:

INSTRUCTIONS

1. In a bowl, combine the tempeh with the marinade ingredients. Toss to coat and let marinate for at least 15 minutes, or up to 30 minutes.

2. Heat a wok or large skillet over high heat. Add the sesame oil.

3. Add the broccoli, bell pepper, carrot, and snow peas to the wok. Stir-fry for 2-3 minutes, or until crisp-tender.

4. Add the marinated tempeh to the wok. Stir-fry for 3-4 minutes, or until browned and heated through.

5. Add the garlic, soy sauce, rice vinegar, and honey to the wok. Stir-fry for 1 minute, or until the sauce is heated through.

6. Combine the vegetables and tempeh with the sauce. Stir-fry for 1 minute more, or until everything is coated in the sauce. Serve immediately over rice.

NOTES

- For a spicier dish, add more red pepper flakes.

- To make this dish gluten-free, use tamari instead of soy sauce.

- Serve over brown rice or cauliflower rice for a complete meal.

NUTRITIONAL INFO (approximate, per serving)

- Calories: 300-350 | Protein: 20-25g | Fat: 15-20g | Carbohydrates: 20-25g | Fiber: 5-7g | Net Carbs: 15-18g

Sweet and Sour Tofu Stir-Fry

A classic Chinese dish, made vegan-friendly with tofu.

 **Prep Time:** 15 minutes || **Cook Time:** 10 minutes || **Yield:** 4 servings

INGREDIENTS

For the marinade:

- 1 block extra-firm tofu, pressed and cubed

- 1 tablespoon soy sauce or tamari

- 1 teaspoon rice vinegar

- 1/2 teaspoon cornstarch

- 1/4 teaspoon red pepper flakes

- 1/4 teaspoon garlic powder

- 1/4 teaspoon ginger powder

For the sweet and sour sauce:

- 1/4 cup pineapple juice

- 1/4 cup ketchup

- 1 tablespoon soy sauce or tamari

- 1 tablespoon rice vinegar

- 1 tablespoon brown sugar or agave nectar

- 1 tablespoon cornstarch

- 1/4 cup water

For the stir-fry:

- 1 bell pepper, sliced

- 1 carrot, sliced

- 1/4 cup broccoli florets

- 1/4 cup snow peas

INSTRUCTIONS

1. In a bowl, combine the tofu cubes with the marinade ingredients. Toss to coat and let marinate for at least 15 minutes, or up to 30 minutes.

2. In a small bowl, whisk together the pineapple juice, ketchup, soy sauce, rice vinegar, brown sugar, cornstarch, and water.

3. Heat a wok or large skillet over high heat. Add the bell pepper, carrot, broccoli, and snow peas, and stir-fry for 2-3 minutes, or until crisp-tender. Remove from the wok and set aside.

4. Return the wok to high heat. Add the marinated tofu and stir-fry for 2-3 minutes, or until browned.

5. Pour the prepared sweet and sour sauce into the wok and bring to a boil. Stir constantly until the sauce thickens and coats the tofu.

6. Return the stir-fried vegetables to the wok and toss to combine. Serve immediately over rice.

NOTES

- For a spicier dish, add more red pepper flakes.

- To make this dish gluten-free, use tamari instead of soy sauce.

- Serve over brown rice or cauliflower rice for a complete meal.

NUTRITIONAL INFO (approximate, per serving)

- Calories: 300-350 | Protein: 20-25g | Fat: 15-20g | Carbohydrates: 20-25g | Fiber: 5-7g | Net Carbs: 15-18g

Spicy Kung Pao Tofu

A classic Chinese dish, revamped for a plant-based and keto-friendly twist.

 **Prep Time:** 15 minutes || **Cook Time:** 10 minutes || **Yield:** 4 servings

INGREDIENTS

For the marinade:

- 1 block extra-firm tofu, pressed and cubed

- 1 tablespoon soy sauce or tamari

- 1 teaspoon rice vinegar

- 1/2 teaspoon cornstarch

- 1/4 teaspoon red pepper flakes

- 1/4 teaspoon garlic powder

- 1/4 teaspoon ginger powder

For the sauce:

- 1 tablespoon sesame oil

- 1 tablespoon chili oil

- 1 clove garlic, minced

- 1 tablespoon grated ginger

- 1/4 cup vegetable broth

- 2 tablespoons soy sauce or tamari

- 1 tablespoon rice vinegar

- 1 tablespoon honey or maple syrup

- 1/2 teaspoon cornstarch

- 1/4 cup chopped peanuts

For the stir-fry:

- 1 bell pepper, sliced

- 1 carrot, sliced

- 1/4 cup broccoli florets

- 1/4 cup snow peas

INSTRUCTIONS

1. In a bowl, combine the tofu cubes with the marinade ingredients. Toss to coat and let marinate for at least 15 minutes, or up to 30 minutes.

2. In a small bowl, whisk together the sesame oil, chili oil, garlic, ginger, vegetable broth, soy sauce, rice vinegar, honey, and cornstarch.

3. Heat a wok or large skillet over high heat. Add the bell pepper, carrot, broccoli, and snow peas, and stir-fry for 2-3 minutes, or until crisp-tender. Remove from the wok and set aside.

4. Return the wok to high heat. Add the marinated tofu and stir-fry for 2-3 minutes, or until browned.

5. Pour the prepared sauce into the wok and bring to a boil. Stir constantly until the sauce thickens and coats the tofu.

6. Return the stir-fried vegetables to the wok and toss to combine. Sprinkle with chopped peanuts and serve immediately.

NOTES

- For a spicier dish, add more red pepper flakes or chili oil.

- To make this dish gluten-free, use tamari instead of soy sauce.

- Serve over brown rice or cauliflower rice for a complete meal.

NUTRITIONAL INFO (approximate, per serving)

- Calories: 300-350 | Protein: 20-25g | Fat: 15-20g | Carbohydrates: 20-25g | Fiber: 5-7g | Net Carbs: 15-18g

CONVERSION GUIDE & MEAL PLANNERS

KITCHEN CONVERSIONS

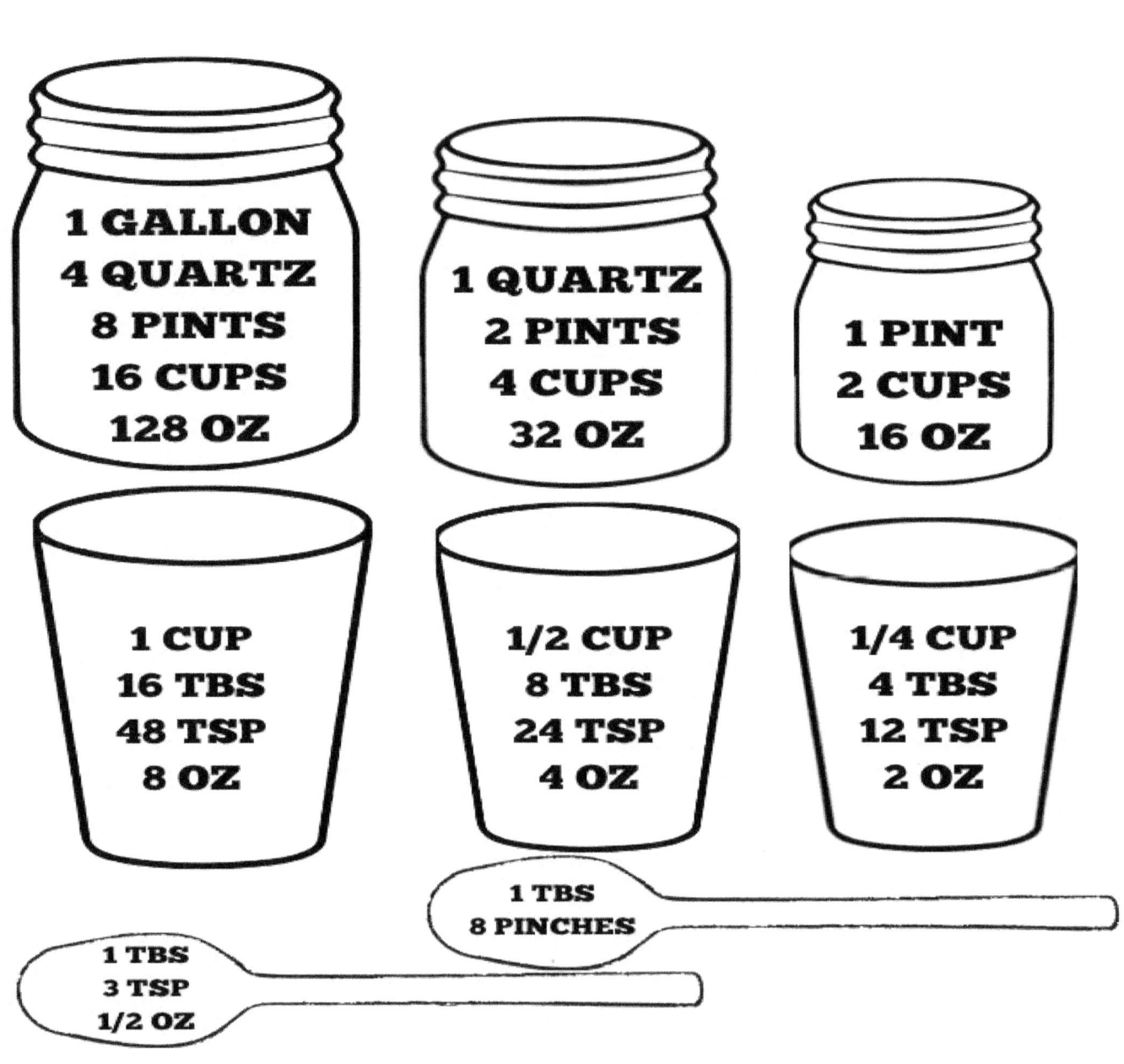

1 GALLON
4 QUARTZ
8 PINTS
16 CUPS
128 OZ

1 QUARTZ
2 PINTS
4 CUPS
32 OZ

1 PINT
2 CUPS
16 OZ

1 CUP
16 TBS
48 TSP
8 OZ

1/2 CUP
8 TBS
24 TSP
4 OZ

1/4 CUP
4 TBS
12 TSP
2 OZ

1 TBS
8 PINCHES

1 TBS
3 TSP
1/2 OZ

Dates

	BREAKFAST	LUNCH	DINNER	SNACKS
MON				
TUE				
WED				
THU				
FRI				
SAT				
SUN				

Shopping list

Dates _____

	BREAKFAST	LUNCH	DINNER	SNACKS
MON				
TUE				
WED				
THU				
FRI				
SAT				
SUN				

Shopping list

_____   _____   _____

_____   _____   _____

_____   _____   _____

_____   _____   _____

_____   _____   _____

Dates
_____

	BREAKFAST	LUNCH	DINNER	SNACKS
MON				
TUE				
WED				
THU				
FRI				
SAT				
SUN				

Shopping list

_____ _____ _____
_____ _____ _____
_____ _____ _____
_____ _____ _____
_____ _____ _____
_____ _____ _____

Dates
_____

	BREAKFAST	LUNCH	DINNER	SNACKS
MON				
TUE				
WED				
THU				
FRI				
SAT				
SUN				

Shopping list

_____ _____ _____

_____ _____ _____

_____ _____ _____

_____ _____ _____

_____ _____ _____

_____ _____ _____

GROCERY LIST

DATE: / /

DAIRY:
- ○ _____
- ○ _____
- ○ _____
- ○ _____
- ○ _____
- ○ _____
- ○ _____
- ○ _____
- ○ _____
- ○ _____
- ○ _____
- ○ _____

MEAT & SEAFOOD:
- ○ _____
- ○ _____
- ○ _____
- ○ _____
- ○ _____
- ○ _____
- ○ _____
- ○ _____
- ○ _____
- ○ _____
- ○ _____
- ○ _____

FRUITS & VEGGIES:
- ○ _____
- ○ _____
- ○ _____
- ○ _____
- ○ _____
- ○ _____
- ○ _____
- ○ _____

BREAD & CEREAL:
- ○ _____
- ○ _____
- ○ _____
- ○ _____
- ○ _____

OTHERS:
- ○ _____
- ○ _____
- ○ _____
- ○ _____
- ○ _____
- ○ _____
- ○ _____
- ○ _____

FROZEN FOODS:
- ○ _____
- ○ _____
- ○ _____
- ○ _____
- ○ _____

CANNED GOODS:
- ○ _____
- ○ _____
- ○ _____
- ○ _____
- ○ _____

WHAT'S COOKING:
- **S**
- **M**
- **T**
- **W**
- **T**
- **F**
- **S**

GROCERY LIST

DATE: / /

DAIRY:
- ○ _____
- ○ _____
- ○ _____
- ○ _____
- ○ _____
- ○ _____
- ○ _____
- ○ _____
- ○ _____
- ○ _____
- ○ _____
- ○ _____

MEAT & SEAFOOD:
- ○ _____
- ○ _____
- ○ _____
- ○ _____
- ○ _____
- ○ _____
- ○ _____
- ○ _____
- ○ _____
- ○ _____
- ○ _____
- ○ _____

FRUITS & VEGGIES:
- ○ _____
- ○ _____
- ○ _____
- ○ _____
- ○ _____
- ○ _____
- ○ _____
- ○ _____

BREAD & CEREAL:
- ○ _____
- ○ _____
- ○ _____
- ○ _____
- ○ _____

OTHERS:
- ○ _____
- ○ _____
- ○ _____
- ○ _____
- ○ _____
- ○ _____
- ○ _____
- ○ _____

FROZEN FOODS:
- ○ _____
- ○ _____
- ○ _____
- ○ _____
- ○ _____

CANNED GOODS:
- ○ _____
- ○ _____
- ○ _____
- ○ _____
- ○ _____

WHAT'S COOKING:
- S _____
- M _____
- T _____
- W _____
- T _____
- F _____
- S _____

Dear Reader,

Thank you for purchasing this cookbook. Creating this cookbook has been a labor of love, and I hope it has inspired you to explore new flavors and techniques in your kitchen. Each recipe has been crafted with care and passion, with the aim to cater to your health and diet requirements.

Your support means the world to me, and I am deeply grateful for your trust in my recipes. As you cook your way through the pages of this book, I hope you find as much joy in making these dishes as I did in creating them.

Jane Garraway

Your Feedback Matters

I would love to hear about your experiences with the recipes in this cookbook. Your honest reviews and feedback are incredibly valuable and help me continue to improve and share the joy of cooking with others. Whether it's a dish that turned out perfectly or one that you think could use some tweaking, your insights are welcomed and appreciated.

Please consider leaving a review on the platform where you purchased this book. Your feedback helps guide future books and ensures that I can continue to provide recipes that resonate with home cooks everywhere.

Thank you once again for your support.

Printed in Great Britain
by Amazon

61487455R00087